FIELDING

Reading and Writing

SECOND EDITION

www.els.edu

Based on materials taken from the following titles:

Focus on Grammar 5: An Integrated Skills Approach, Third Edition, Jay Maurer
For Your Information 1: Basic Reading Skills, Karen Blanchard and Christine Root
For Your Information 2: Intermediate Reading Skills, Karen Blanchard and Christine Root
Introduction to Academic Writing, Second Edition, Alice Oshima and Ann Hogue
More Reading Power: Reading with Pleasure, Comprehension Skills, Thinking Skills, Reading Faster, Second Edition, Beatrice S. Mikulecky and Linda Jeffries
Password 3: A Reading and Vocabulary Text, Lynn Bonesteel
Read Ahead 1: Reading and Life Skills Development, Jo McEntire
Read Ahead 2: Reading and Life Skills Development, Jo McEntire
Reading Power: Reading with Pleasure, Comprehension Skills, Thinking Skills, Reading Faster, Third Edition, Beatrice S. Mikulecky and Linda Jeffries
Ready to Read More: A Skills-Based Reader, Karen Blanchard and Christine Root
Ready to Write More: From Paragraph to Essay, Second Edition, Karen Blanchard and Christine Root
Writing to Communicate: Paragraphs and Essays, Second Edition, Cynthia A. Boardman and Jia Frydenberg

Excerpts taken from:

Ready to Write More: From Paragraph to Essay, Second Edition
by Karen Blanchard and Christine Root
Copyright © 2004 by Pearson Education, Inc.
Published by Addison Wesley Longman
White Plains, NY 10606
ISBN: 0-13-048468-7

Reading Power: Reading with Pleasure, Comprehension Skills, Thinking Skills, Reading Faster, Third Edition
by Beatrice S. Mikulecky and Linda Jeffries
Copyright © 2005 by Pearson Education, Inc.
Published by Addison Wesley Longman
ISBN: 0-13-130548-4

For Your Information 2: Intermediate Reading Skills
by Karen Blanchard and Christine Root
Copyright © 1997 by Addison Wesley Publishing Company, Inc.
A Pearson Education Company
ISBN: 0-201-82538-4

Read Ahead 2: Reading and Life Skills Development
by Jo McEntire
Copyright © 2004 by Pearson Education, Inc.
Published by Addison Wesley Longman
ISBN: 0-13-111784-X

Password 3: A Reading and Vocabulary Text
by Lynn Bonesteel
Copyright © 2005 by Pearson Education, Inc.
Published by Addison Wesley Longman
ISBN: 0-13-140893-3

Read Ahead 1: Reading and Life Skills Development
by Jo McEntire
Copyright © 2005 by Pearson Education, Inc.
Published by Addison Wesley Longman
ISBN: 0-13-118947-6

Writing to Communicate: Paragraphs and Essays, Second Edition
by Cynthia A. Boardman and Jia Frydenberg
Copyright © 2002 by Pearson Education, Inc.
Published by Addison Wesley Longman
ISBN: 0-13-027254-X

Introduction to Academic Writing, Second Edition
by Alice Oshima and Ann Hogue
Copyright © 1997 by Addison Wesley Longman
ISBN: 0-201-69509-X

For Your Information 1: Basic Reading Skills
by Karen Blanchard and Christine Root
Copyright © 1996 by Addison Wesley Publishing Company, Inc.
A Pearson Education Company
ISBN: 0-201-83409-X

Ready to Read More: A Skills-Based Reader
by Karen Blanchard and Christine Root
Copyright © 2006 by Pearson Education, Inc.
Published by Addison Wesley Longman
ISBN: 0-13-177649-5

More Reading Power: Reading with Pleasure, Comprehension Skills, Thinking Skills, Reading Faster, Second Edition
by Beatrice S. Mikulecky and Linda Jeffries
Copyright © 2004 by Pearson Education, Inc.
Published by Addison Wesley Longman
ISBN: 0-13-061199-9

Focus on Grammar 5: An Integrated Skills Approach, Third Edition
by Jay Maurer
Copyright ©2006, 2000, 1994 by Pearson Education, Inc.
Published by Addison Wesley Longman
ISBN: 0-13-191275-5

This special edition published in cooperation with Pearson Custom Publishing.

Printed in the United States of America

11 12 V013 14 13 12 11

Please visit our web site at *www.pearsoncustom.com*

ISBN 0-536-29984-6

2005240455

EM

PEARSON CUSTOM PUBLISHING
75 Arlington Street, Suite 300, Boston, MA 02116
A Pearson Education Company

Sequence Chart Fielding

Unit	Reading Skills	Writing Skills	Rhetorical Skills	Vocabulary
1	Vocabulary guessing strategies; understanding main ideas and major points; supporting details; skimming; analyzing a problem/solution essay	Brainstorming; writing about solutions to problems; organizing a problem/solution essay	Problem/solution	Words related to sleep; word families
2	Scanning; identifying the main idea and supporting ideas; previewing/predicting			Words related to business; idioms and expressions
3	Using context clues; recognizing similarities; analyzing a comparison/contrast essay	Writing about comparison/contrast; organizing a comparison/contrast essay	Comparison/contrast	Words related to movies; expressions of comparison/contrast
4	Previewing; using context clues; reading fiction			Words related to tests; words related to anxiety
Appendices	Pleasure reading	Paraphrasing and summarizing; organizing an essay; punctuation		Linking words

Acknowledgments

On behalf of ELS Educational Services, Inc., I would like to express our thanks to the 2006 Curriculum Committee. While there were many people involved at every level of our organization, we will list, for the sake of space and time considerations, those who were most able to devote significant time to the effort.

Revising content from previous editions was the "Content Replacement" task force: Terri Rapoport, Marjorie Friedman, Catherine Flores, Judy Dillon, Marie Silva, Ellen Clegg, Peggy Street, Brigit Solé-March, Catherine Mason and Christine Thelen. Ward Morrow, Susan Matson and Morgan Foster facilitated the process, helped with selections, and coordinated the results.

Ferreting out typos and inconsistencies was the "Cleanup Crew": Terri Rapoport, Ward Morrow, Morgan Foster, Yasmine Bia, Abel Hassan, and Susan Matson. Ellen Clegg helped with transitional material and Jim Scofield commented on level appropriateness.

Much-needed note taking components were added to levels 109 and Masters with the able assistance of Shane O'Brien, Terri Rapoport, Brigit Solé-March, Jill Shafer, Linda Lindstrom and Susan Matson. Tim Hancock, Eric Dean and many other Academic Directors gave very detailed piloting feedback.

Other task forces continue, as of this writing, with support areas such as a recreation of the Language Activity Chart, with the help of Dan Manolescu; adjustments to final exams, with the assistance of Bonnie Olson; and the development of teachers' manuals, guided by Peggy Street.

Overseas Academic Directors who coordinated the piloting of the materials in their centers included Robert Baker (Japan—Tokyo), Kieran Culhane (Japan—Sapporo), P. K. Lim (Malaysia), and Yasmine Bia (Vancouver).

First in the greater scheme of teaching excellence are the many instructors in 43 Centers who tried out the new materials, provided constructive criticism and gave helpful advice.

Finally, thank you to all our academic staff and students for your belief in the power of teaching and learning English—and helping our world communicate better. May we all contribute to more peace, friendship, and understanding among all countries of the world.

Mark W. Harris
President and CEO
ELS Language Centers

Introduction

We at ELS Language Centers are proud to present our 2007 edition Reading and Writing textbooks. These books are used for a portion of the day in our Intensive and Semi-Intensive programs and are complemented by texts and materials in Structure and Speaking Practice, Language Technology Center and Skills Enhancement classes.

There are three stages in the ELS Language Centers Reading and Writing curriculum—Beginning, Intermediate and Advanced—and each stage consists of three levels, low to high.

Our focus in creating the textbooks has been to create active rather than passive readers and writers through the practice of reading, summarizing, sharing and reflecting in both oral and written forms.

In designing these texts, we used a variety of resources to provide learners with authentic readings of high interest and appeal, with various tasks to improve reading comprehension and speed. The topics were chosen to stimulate discussion and thought and act as a platform for written expression. These texts include clear models of various rhetorical writing styles and explanations, as well as practice of grammatical structures and mechanics.

Contents

Unit One

Problem Solving

Section I: Reading

Why Read Faster?

There are three important reasons for learning to read faster:

- You can read more in less time.
- You can understand more.
- You can learn to think in English.

How is it possible to understand more when you read faster? The answer is very simple: When you read slowly, you read one word at a time. This way, you read separate words like the words below. Is it easier or harder to understand these sentences?

> What really happens when we read? Some people think we read one word at a time. They think we read a word, understand it, and then move on to the next word.

Reading separate words makes it harder to understand. The separate words become separate pieces of information. It's hard to remember lots of separate pieces of information. You may not remember the beginning of a sentence when you get to the end!

When you read faster, you read groups of words. Then your memory can work better because you are reading phrases or small ideas. It's easier to remember these ideas than a lot of separate words. It's also easier to connect these ideas together. Then you can get the larger, general idea of what you are reading. This is why you can understand better when you read faster.

Reading phrases or groups of words also helps you learn to think in English. That's because your brain is understanding ideas, not words.

The following selection will assist you in determining your reading rate and in setting your reading goals. Throughout the text, you will practice various techniques to increase your speed and improve your comprehension. There will be a final reading in the last unit to help you assess your progress and to plan your future objectives.

READING RATE TABLE

Reading Time (Minutes: Seconds)	Rate (Words per Minute)	Reading Time (Minutes: Seconds)	Rate (Words per Minute)
:30 sec	800 wpm		
:35	686	2:10	185
:40	597	2:15	178
:45	533	2:20	172
:50	480	2:25	166
:55	440	2:30	160
1:00	400	2:35	155
1:05	370	2:40	149
1:10	345	2:45	145
1:15	320	2:50	141
1:20	300	2:55	137
1:25	282	3:00	133
1:30	267	3:15	123
1:35	253	3:30	114
1:40	240	3:45	107
1:45	229	4:00	100
1:50	219	4:15	94
1:55	209	4:30	89
2:00	200	4:45	84
2:05	192	5:00	80

Timed Reading

Fear of Flying

Starting time ________

Are you afraid of flying on a plane? If you are, you're not alone. About one in four people is afraid of flying. That number increases every time there is a terrible plane crash or a war. But for many people, the fear is always there.

Some of these people fly anyway. They have a few drinks, or they take some medicine. During the flight, they try to forget they are on a plane. For others, the problem is worse. Even the thought of sitting on a plane makes them anxious. If they get on a plane, they can become ill from fear. They may become so ill that they have to get off the plane before it leaves.

In fact, there are really very few accidents with planes. Airline companies check their planes carefully before every flight. If the pilot thinks there is any problem with the plane, it doesn't take off. This means that accidents are very unlikely. The United States National Safety Council says that flying in a plane is much less dangerous than riding in a car. But these facts don't matter to the people who are afraid.

Scientists say that there are two different types of fear of flying. The first is the fear of falling out of the sky. Since the terrorist attacks of September 11, 2001, more people suffer from this fear. They think about all the bad things that could possibly happen. And they can think of lots of bad things that can happen to a plane high in the sky. The second type is a fear of being in a closed place. People with this fear never want to be in closed places. On a plane, they are afraid they might be trapped. If anything happens, they might not be able to get out.

For some fearful travellers, there may be only one solution. They have to travel on the ground—by car, bus, train, or boat. Other people, however, need to travel by air. In this case, they'll have to find some way to get over their fear. Doctors and scientists say it's not easy, but it's possible. They say that the important thing is not to give up flying. There are several ways to do this. Some airline companies offer one-day courses for people who are afraid of flying. In many cities, hospitals or doctors also offer special courses for these people.

(400 words)

Finishing time ____________ **Reading time** ____________

Answer the questions on the following page.

Reading/Writing—Fielding

Circle the best answer. Do not look back!

1. This passage is about
   a. courses for people with a fear of flying.
   b. what happens to people on a plane.
   c. why people don't like traveling.
   d. how some people are afraid of flying.
2. Fear of flying is a problem for
   a. many people.
   b. only a few people.
   c. people in Europe.
   d. doctors and scientists.
3. Some people are so afraid on a plane that they
   a. call a doctor.
   b. watch a movie.
   c. become ill.
   d. talk to themselves.
4. Flying in a plane is
   a. safer than riding in a car.
   b. not as safe as riding in a car.
   c. not as safe as riding a bicycle.
   d. safer than flying in a balloon.
5. According to scientists, some people are afraid the plane
   a. won't take off.
   b. won't be on time.
   c. will fall down.
   d. will land badly.
6. Other people are afraid they
   a. won't have good food on the plane.
   b. will be trapped in the plane.
   c. may get sick on the plane.
   d. might take the wrong plane.
7. If you're afraid of flying, you
   a. shouldn't watch the news.
   b. can travel on the ground.
   c. can't ever travel anywhere.
   d. should probably stay home.
8. Doctors say it's important not to
   a. give up flying.
   b. fly on small planes.
   c. travel by car and train.
   d. take lots of medicine.

Reading A: Sleepy Teens

Why is this teenager so sleepy?

Getting Ready to Read

A. Complete the activity below. Then, talk with a partner or in a small group about the results.

Walk around the class, and ask your classmates about their sleeping habits. Try to find at least one person for each category. Write their names in the chart. Ask your classmates if they are happy with their sleep habits. If not, what would they like to change?

Gets enough sleep	Doesn't get enough sleep	Falls asleep during class	Sleeps less than 6 hours a night	Sleeps more than 8 hours a night	Likes to take naps	Usually goes to bed before 10:00

*B .The **boldfaced** words and phrases below appear in the reading. Which words are new to you? Circle them. Then, work with a partner. Read the definitions of the words, and complete the sentences next to each picture with the words.*

experiment = a scientific test done to find out how something or someone will react in a particular situation, or to find out if a theory is true
patterns = regularly repeated arrangement of shapes, lines, or colors on a surface
in tears = crying
depressed = feeling very unhappy

1. The researchers in the sleep laboratory are doing an ______________. They want to find out if teenagers' brains are active when they are sleeping.
2. They are checking the brain wave ______________ of the people who are sleeping.

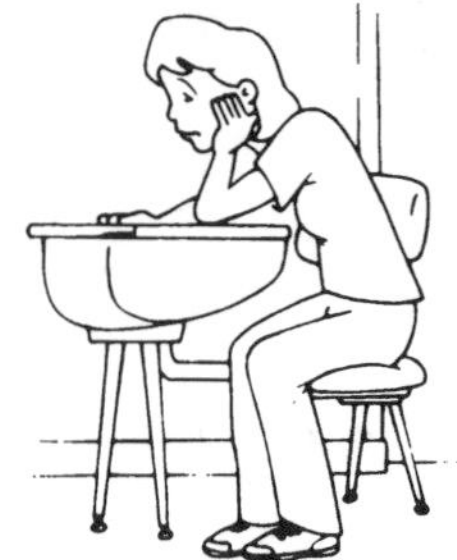

3. Like many other teenagers, this girl is ______________. Sleep researchers think that it might be because she is not getting enough sleep.

4. This boy tried to go to bed at 8:30. He is ______________ because he is upset that he can't fall asleep.

Reading

Read the text once without stopping.

Sleepy Teens

1 When school superintendent[1] Russell Dever enters the local coffee shop at around 7:20 A.M., it is crowded with students. "The line is out the door because our high school kids are getting coffee," he said.

2 And they are not standing in line for the decaf[2]—they need the caffeine[3] to stay awake in class. Talk to American high school students and you hear the **complaints** about how late they **stay up**, how little they sleep—and how early they must be in class.

3 These days, there is increasing **concern** in schools across the United States about students who are not completely awake in morning classes. School **officials** in some states have even changed start times so teenagers can sleep later.

4 According to sleep **expert** Mary Carskadon, the fact that many teenagers work long hours outside of school and have computers and televisions in their bedrooms contributes to a serious **lack** of sleep. But, she said, the problem is also due to biology.[4] As the bodies of teenagers develop, their brains also change. These changes make teens more **likely** than adults to have trouble sleeping at night.

5 Teenagers need **at least** eight to nine hours of sleep a night, but the average teen gets a lot less. Carskadon's study, completed in the fall of 2001 with researcher Amy Wolfson, showed that nearly 30 percent of students in the tenth grade slept less than six hours on school nights. Less than 15 percent got more than eight hours of sleep each night. Eighth-graders averaged eight hours of sleep a night, although that age group, she said, needs at least nine hours a night.

[1]a **school superintendent** someone who is responsible for all of the schools in a particular area of the United States

[2]**decaf** short form of the phrase *decaffeinated coffee,* coffee that has had the caffeine removed

[3]**caffeine** the chemical substance in coffee, tea, and some other drinks that makes people feel more active

[4]**biology** the scientific study of living things

6 Even more remarkable are the results of a 1997–1998 school year study. In that study, 12 out of 24 U.S. high school students who were part of an **experiment** at a sleep laboratory had brain wave **patterns** similar to those of someone with narcolepsy, a serious condition that affects sleep. "What's going on is that at 8:30 in the morning these kids . . . would normally be in school sitting in a classroom, but . . . their brain is still in the middle of the night," said Carskadon.

7 Parent Dawn Dow says her 12-year-old son just cannot go to bed before 10 P.M. "Last year he was trying to put himself to bed at 8:30 and was coming in at 9:30 and 10 **in tears** saying, 'I just can't go to sleep.' It is not a case of children wanting to be up late . . . . It is a change in his chemistry."

8 So would letting teenagers wake up later make a difference? Kyla Wahlstrom of the University of Minnesota in the United States studies the effects of earlier school start times. She has looked at students in Edina and Minneapolis, two cities in Minnesota, where public school officials have moved high school starting times past 8:30 A.M. In Minneapolis, the middle school begins at 9:30 A.M. She said the later starting times have **reduced** student **absences**. They have also lowered **dropout** rates by 8 percent over four years. In addition, she said, teachers report that students are not sleeping at their desks during the first two hours of class anymore. She said 92 percent of parents from Edina reported that their teenagers are easier to live with. The students reported that they were feeling less **depressed** and were getting better grades.

9 Big changes in school start times may not be possible in some areas. However, Wahlstrom said her research shows that even small changes can contribute to a solution to this serious problem.

Notes

Mary Carskadon is professor of psychiatry[5] and human behavior at Brown University in Providence, Rhode Island, U.S.A. and director of sleep and chronobiology[6] at Bradley Hospital in East Providence, Rhode Island, U.S.A.

Amy Wolfson is a researcher at the College of the Holy Cross in Worcester, Massachusetts, U.S.A.

Kyla Wahlstrom is associate director[7] of the Center for Applied Research and Educational Improvement at the University of Minnesota, U.S.A.

[5]**psychiatry** the study and treatment of mental illness
[6]**chronobiology** the study of the effects of time on living things
[7]**associate director** someone who assists the director

Comprehension Check

Read these sentences. Circle T (true) or F (false). If you circle F, change the sentence to make it true. Check your answers with a classmate. If your answers are different, look back at the reading.

1. Often, teenagers sleep more than they should. T F
2. There are scientific reasons that explain why teenagers have difficulty sleeping at night. T F
3. The brains of teenagers are the same as the brains of adults. T F
4. Teenagers can do their best schoolwork in the early morning. T F
5. It's easier for adults to fall asleep at night than teenagers. T F
6. Some schools start their classes later so that teenage students can get more sleep in the morning. T F

Exploring Vocabulary

Thinking about the Vocabulary

Guessing Strategy

Often, writers don't want to repeat a word, so they use a **synonym**. Synonyms are words that have similar meanings. If you don't know a word, look at the sentences nearby to see if there is a synonym. Look at the example.

> Some students who don't get enough sleep get **depressed**. And because they feel so unhappy, they can't concentrate on their schoolwork.

Based on the context, you can guess that the words *depressed* and *unhappy* are similar in meaning.

Try It!

Circle the word in the second sentence that is a synonym for the **boldfaced** target word.

> She said the later starting times have **reduced** student absences. They have also lowered dropout rates by 8 percent over four years.

Look at the target words and phrases. Which ones are new to you? Circle them here and in the reading. Then read "Sleepy Teens" again. Look at the context of each new word and phrase. Can you guess the meaning? Use the Guessing Strategy where possible.

Target Words and Phrases

complaints (2)	**expert** (4)	**experiment** (6)	**absences** (8)
stay up (2)	**lack** (4)	**patterns** (6)	**dropout** (8)
concern (3)	**likely** (4)	**in tears** (7)	**depressed** (8)
officials (3)	**at least** (5)	**reduced** (8)	

Using the Vocabulary

These sentences are **about the reading.** Complete them with the words and phrases in the box. Circle the words or phrases in the sentences that help you understand the meanings of the target words.

absences	at least	complaint	concern	dropout	experts
lack	likely	official	reduced	stay up	

1. Russell Dever is a school ________. He is responsible for several schools.
2. High school students ________ late at night, so they have trouble waking up early to go to school.
3. A common ________ from young people is that they don't get enough sleep. They are unhappy that school begins so early in the morning.
4. Some parents and school officials are worried that many high school students are too tired to learn. Because of their ________, some school officials have decided to change the time when high school classes start.
5. Researchers who study human sleep patterns say that teenagers get much less sleep than they really need. According to these ________, there are many different reasons for this serious ________ of sleep.

6. The main reason that teenagers are more ________ to have trouble sleeping than adults is due to the fact that their bodies are changing.
7. Most teenagers need ________ eight hours of sleep a night. In fact, it's even better if they get nine or ten hours.
8. When teenagers don't get enough sleep, they are more likely to miss class. In one school where start times were changed from 8:30 A.M. to 9:30 A.M., there are now fewer ________. The later start times seem to have ________ the number of students who don't go to class because they can't wake up in the morning.
9. The later start times have also lowered the ________ rate. This means that fewer students are quitting school.

Developing Reading Skills

Understanding Main Ideas, Major Points, and Supporting Details

A reading generally has one **main idea**, with several **major points** to support it. Those major points are supported by **supporting details**. For example, in "Sleepy Teens" there is one main idea, three major points to support it, and many supporting details to illustrate the major points.

Answer these questions.

1. What is the main idea of "Sleepy Teens"?
   a. Some schools in the United States are experimenting with later school start times because experts say that teenagers will be happier and do better in school if they get more sleep.
   b. Many teenagers have difficulty falling asleep at night because of the biological changes in their brains and because they have televisions and computers in their rooms.
   c. Most American teenagers are depressed because they do not get enough sleep.
2. Which of these sentences are major points and which are supporting details? Write MP (major point) or SD (supporting detail).

   __MP__ 1. There are many reasons that teenagers have trouble sleeping at night.

   _____ 2. Research shows that many teenagers do not get enough sleep.

   _____ 3. Many teenagers work long hours outside school.

   _____ 4. Thirty percent of students in the tenth grade sleep less than six hours on school nights.

   _____ 5. Schools that are experimenting with later start times are happy with the results.

   _____ 6. There are biological changes in the brains of teenagers that make it difficult for them to fall asleep at night.

_____ 7. In one school that changed its start time from 8:30 to 9:30 A.M., the number of student absences has gone down.

_____ 8. The students feel less depressed and get better grades when they get enough sleep.

Expanding Vocabulary

Using the Vocabulary in New Contexts

These sentences use the target words and phrases in new contexts. Complete them with the words and phrases in the box.

absences	at least	complaint	concern	dropout	expert
lack	likely	official	reduce	stay up	

1. She has written more than ten books on education. She is an _________ on the subject.
2. I don't remember exactly how much money I have in the bank, but I know it's _________ $500. I might have more. I'll have to call the bank to check.
3. I'm going to take a nap so that I can _________ late to watch that TV special.
4. Take your umbrella. The weather report said that rain is _________ later this afternoon.
5. The service in that restaurant was terrible. I'm going to write a letter of _________ to the manager.
6. Thank you for your _________, but I'm fine. Don't worry about me.
7. If you want to lose weight, you must _________ the amount of food that you eat.
8. They are concerned about their son's complete _________ of interest in his studies. He doesn't seem to be interested in any subject.
9. You have too many _________. You need to make sure you attend all of the rest of the classes, or you will have to repeat the course.
10. My town has a serious _________ problem. Students are leaving high school early and can't find jobs.
11. He works for the government. He is the _________ who is responsible for public safety.

Word Families

A. Many words can be nouns, verbs, or adjectives. Look back at the reading. How are the target words below used? Write N (noun), V (verb), or A (adjective).

____ absence	____ complaint	____ concern	____ depressed
____ dropout	____ experiment	____ official	____ reduced

B. In the paragraph below, circle the words that are related to the target words from Exercise A. Then complete the chart with the words you circled.

It's 7:20 A.M., and teenagers are standing in line on the sidewalk in front of the local coffee shop. They complain that school starts too early in the morning, so they have to drink coffee to stay awake in class. They also complain of being depressed. Some students are absent because they can't wake up, and students who are absent a lot are more likely to drop out of school. This concerns many parents and school officials, so some schools are experimenting with a change in school start times. They hope that if teens can sleep a little later in the morning, they will be able to pay better attention in class. They also hope that the later start times will result in a reduction in the number of students who miss class. And some teens are reporting that their depression has disappeared since they started getting more sleep. If the experiment works, the schools will probably make the change official.

Noun	Verb	Adjective
	complain	

Reading B:

Skim this magazine article to get the general ideas. Remember, you need to read only a few sentences and words. Read as quickly as you can. Then, answer the questions below.

BURNING TREES TO SAVE A FOREST

by Liz Westfield

Burning trees to save a forest! Strange as it sounds, that is the United States Forest Service's new idea for saving America's forests.

For more than a hundred years, Americans were taught that fires in a forest were always bad. When trees burned in the forest, it was a disaster which would ruin the forest. The Forest Service promoted this idea in many ways. They even invented a character named Smokey the Bear, who always said, "Remember, only *you* can prevent forest fires."

In the past, whenever there was a fire in the forest, the rangers immediately put it out. No fires were allowed to burn, even in places where many of the trees, were dead or diseased. This did not help the forests, however. In fact, with so many dead and diseased trees, the forest fires in the western United States have been far worse in recent years.

The new chief of the U.S. Forest Service recently explained that there is a new and better way to save our forests. He said, "Small, limited fires are part of nature. That is the way that old, dead, and diseased trees are cleared away to make room for new trees."

Now the Forest Service has new plans. They will start small fires in forests, but they will control the fires. The fires will be started in parts of the forest which are old and full of diseased trees. The rangers plan to burn about 30,000 acres a year for the next 20 years.

As the chief said, "It took many years for the forests to become old and diseased, and so it will take more than 20 years to correct the problem by using controlled fires."

1. In the past, what did Americans think about forest fires?
2. What happened in the past when there was a forest fire?
3. What is the new plan of the Forest Service?

Show your answers to another student. Do you have the same answers? Check your answers by reading the whole article.

Reading C:

Skim this magazine article to get the general ideas. Remember, you need to read only a few sentences and words. Read as quickly as you can. Then, answer the questions below.

SOME PROBLEMS WITH E-MAIL AT WORK

by Yuki Shibata

Everyone knows the advantages of using e-mail. It's much faster than ordinary mail. It's much cheaper than the telephone. And it's easier than trying to meet with someone in person. However, it is not always good to use e-mail at work. Some companies are limiting the use of e-mail in their offices for several reasons.

One reason is that e-mail is only one-way. You send out your message and then you have to wait for an answer. This is not a problem if you need to send simple information. You may only need to know that the message was received. But if the message is more complicated, e-mail is not so good. It's not good, for example, if you need to make a decision or a plan. It can take many messages and a lot of time to decide something by e-mail. In that case, it's better to talk on the phone. Or, if you're in the same building, you should go meet in person. Then you can also take a little walk and you can get to know each other better.

There is another problem with e-mail: You don't get much information from the message. You have only the words themselves. This doesn't matter if the message is just about facts or if it is not important. But it might cause trouble if the message is about something important. You can't tell much about the person who sent the message. You have no idea what she was thinking or feeling. You may put your own feelings into the message. And this can lead to communication problems in a company.

In England, psychologists did some research about using e-mail at work. They studied office workers opening their e-mail. The psychologists measured the blood pressure of the workers. They found that certain kinds of messages made blood pressure go up. It went up if the messages seemed angry or negative. It also went up if the messages were from the boss. It went up the highest when the messages were both negative and from the boss.

The psychologists said that people should be careful how they use e-mail at work. This is especially true for the people with top jobs in a company. Their messages can easily hurt or upset people. They should never send important news by e-mail. They should always meet face to face with the person. Then everyone will understand each other better and will work together better.

1. What are some problems with e-mail at work?
2. What did psychologists in England do research about?
3. Why should people be careful about using e-mail?

Show your answers to another student. Do you have the same answers? Check your answers by reading the whole article.

Unit One Above material from: *Reading Power*

Section II: Writing the Problem/Solution Essay

When your purpose is to describe a problem and evaluate possible solutions, you will write a **problem/solution** essay. For example, if you are discussing solutions to the problem of employee dissatisfaction in your company or the problems of adjusting to a foreign culture, you would write this type of essay. You should organize your solutions according to order of importance.

The problem/solution pattern is very useful in academic writing. For example, you would use it in a sociology class if you were asked to talk about solutions to the problem of teen pregnancy. You could also write this type of essay in an economics class if you needed to suggest some ways to solve the unemployment problem in your city.

Brainstorming Solutions

For each of the problems described below, think of at least three possible solutions. Work in small groups, and then compare your solutions with those of your classmates.

1. Living in a foreign country can be fun and exciting, but it can also be problematic. One of the most serious problems that people living in a foreign country face is culture shock. What ways can you think of to help people deal with this problem?

   Problem: Culture shock

   Solutions:

   a. *Keep in touch with your family and friends at home.*

   b. ______________________________

   c. ______________________________

2. Many people have trouble falling asleep or staying asleep for an adequate amount of time. This problem is known as insomnia. What suggestions would you give to people who cannot seem to get a good night's sleep?

Problem: Insomnia

Solutions:

a. ______________________________

b. ______________________________

c. ______________________________

3. Stress at work or school can be a serious problem. A person suffering from too much stress usually finds it difficult to be productive or happy. What are some ways to reduce the amount of stress in someone's life?

Problem: Stress at work or school

Solutions:

a. ______________________________

b. ______________________________

c. ______________________________

4. The population of the world keeps growing. Every fifteen seconds, approximately 100 babies are born. Experts predict that by the year 2015, there will be 7 billion people on our planet. By the end of the century, the population could reach 10 billion people. The problem is that there probably will not be enough food to feed everyone. What solutions can you come up with to help solve this problem?

Problem: Overpopulation

Solutions:

a. ______________________________

b. ______________________________

c. ______________________________

5. Illiteracy is a serious problem all over the world. For example, one-third of adults in the United States are functionally illiterate. People who cannot read and write have many disadvantages functioning in society. What solutions can you come up with to help overcome this problem?

   Problem: Illiteracy

   Solutions:

   a. ____

   b. ____

   c. ____

6. Many of the Earth's resources are nonrenewable and will eventually run out. In order to make our valuable natural resources last longer, we need to conserve materials and recycle them as much as possible. Unfortunately, it is not always easy to convince people of the necessity of recycling. What ideas do you have about getting people to recycle?

   Problem: Getting people to recycle

   Solutions:

   a. ____

   b. ____

   c. ____

Offering Solutions

You are the advice consultant for a newspaper. How would you respond to the following letters? Be sure to offer several solutions to each problem in your response. Share your responses by exchanging papers with your classmates or by reading them out loud.

Dear Advisor,

When I first came to the United States to study Western literature, I never dreamed I would fall in love—especially with an American. I had planned to spend two years here getting my master's degree and then return to Japan and teach. Now, only nine months later, everything has changed. I met Jim in one of my classes, and we started studying together. One thing led to the next, and before I knew it, I was engaged. It wasn't exactly love at first sight, but almost. Jim's parents are wonderful. They say that they would love to have a Japanese daughter-in-law. Unfortunately, my parents are a different story. They can't accept the fact that I would marry someone who isn't Japanese. They are very upset and want me to forget about Jim and all our plans for a wedding when we graduate. In fact, they are urging me to come home at the end of the semester and spend the summer in Japan. They think that I'll get over Jim if I don't see him for three months.

I'm so confused. I'm really close to my parents and don't want to hurt them. On the other hand, I love Jim and want to spend the rest of my life with him. I think I would be happy living in the United States, but I'm afraid my parents would never get over it. What suggestions do you have for me? HELP!!

Confused

Dear Confused,

____

____

____

____

____

Dear Advisor,

I'm a sophomore in college. Last year my roommate, Fred, and I were very good friends. I don't know what happened, but this year everything has changed. Fred seems really different. He has a whole new group of friends and spends all of his time with them. He stays out late at night and often doesn't get up in time for his classes. He never studies any more, and he got kicked off the wrestling team for missing so many practices. He's always either sleeping or out with his new friends. When he's in our room, he is moody, messy, and undependable. Please tell me what to do. I've tried talking to him, but he just tells me to mind my own business. I'm concerned that he's going to get kicked out of school. He's already on academic probation. What should I do?

A Concerned Roommate

Dear Concerned,

____

____

____

____

____

____

Work with a Partner

On a separate piece of paper, write your own letter to the advice consultant. You can write about a real problem that you have or make one up. Then exchange letters with a classmate and write a response.

MODEL Problem/Solution Essay

Read the essay below.

Energy Sources: A Dilemma for the Twenty-First Century

All of us have come to expect that reliable sources of energy will be available forever. We drive our cars wherever and whenever we want. When the gas tank gets low, we simply pull into the nearest gas station. At home, whenever we need to change the temperature, prepare food, listen to music, or watch TV, we simply turn on the nearest appliance. What is the source of all this energy that we use so carelessly? In most of the world, energy is created by burning fossil fuels—coal, natural gas, and oil. The problem is that these resources are finite. At our current rate of use, by the year 2080, the world's supply of oil will be almost gone. That means that if you are under the age of forty, the day will probably come when you will not have *enough* gasoline for your car or electricity for your appliances. The three most commonly proposed solutions to this worldwide problem are increasing the efficiency of appliances and vehicles, improving conservation efforts, and finding alternative energy sources.

The first solution, increasing the efficiency of appliances and vehicles, is something that manufacturers have been working on for three decades. For instance, televisions now use 65 to 75 percent less electricity than they did in the 1970s, refrigerators use 20 to 30 percent less electricity, and cars need less gas to travel more miles. Unfortunately, there are so many more televisions, refrigerators, and cars in the world now that overall consumption continues to rise.

Another solution to the dangerous energy situation is to improve our conservation efforts. For example, all of us must get in the habit of recycling whatever we can. We have to install high-efficiency light bulbs in our homes and offices and turn off the lights in rooms that we are not using. It would also help if we biked, walked, carpooled, or used public transportation more and used our cars less. Unfortunately, improvements in both conservation and efficiency are only temporary solutions. They extend the useful life of our current fuels, but they do not explain what we will do when these fuels run out.

The best solution, then, is to find alternative sources of energy to meet our future needs. The current leading alternatives to fossil fuels are fusion and solar energy. Fusion is a nuclear reaction that results in an enormous release of energy. It is practically pollution-free and is probably our best long-range option. Unfortunately, it will not be available for at least twenty years. The other possible energy source, solar power, is the source of all energy, except nuclear, on Earth. When people think of solar energy, they generally think of the many ways that individual homeowners can utilize the power of the sun for heating water and buildings. But solar energy can also be utilized to generate electricity and to purify fuels for automobiles.

It is clear that for us to have sufficient energy resources for the twenty-first century, it will be necessary to pursue the development and encourage the use of alternative energy sources worldwide. If we ignore this problem, what will become of our children? What will life be like for them in the year 2050?

Work with a Partner

Answer the following questions with a partner.

1. What is the thesis statement of the essay?
2. What three solutions to the energy shortage does the author propose?
3. What examples does the author use to describe each solution?
4. How are the supporting paragraphs arranged within the essay?
5. What technique(s) did the author use in writing the conclusion?

Essay Plan: Problem/Solution

The guidelines below will help you remember what you need to do in each part of a problem/solution essay.

Introduction

1. Describe the problem and state why it is serious.
2. Write a thesis statement that identifies possible solutions.

Supporting Paragraphs

1. Discuss one solution in each supporting paragraph.
2. Provide details to explain each solution.
3. Organize the paragraphs according to order of importance.

Conclusion

1. Summarize the solutions.
2. Draw a conclusion or make a prediction based on your suggestions.

Writing Problem/Solution Essays

Read the case below about Tom Higgins's restaurant, The Undergrad Grill. In this activity, you will focus on solutions.

On April 15, Tom Higgins opened a new restaurant at Benson University. He called it the Undergrad Grill. Tom had wanted to open a restaurant at Benson for several months but was waiting for the right location to become available. He was very pleased when he was able to rent suitable space on Restaurant Row. He figured that this would be a great location and well worth the high rent and all the renovations he needed to do on the building. Since he wanted to open the restaurant as soon as possible, he hired the first people he could find to do the renovations and painting. He ended up overpaying the workers because he wanted to get the job done as quickly as possible. When the time came to open, he didn't have enough money to do much advertising. However, since his restaurant was surrounded by many other restaurants and since over 25,000 undergraduate and graduate students were looking for a place to eat, Higgins was certain his restaurant would do well even without advertising. After placing several help-wanted ads in the local newspaper, Higgins hired two waitresses to work for him. He couldn't afford professional cooks, so he hired several students to do the cooking.

UNDERGRAD GRILL

Open 11 A.M. to 11 P.M.

Soups

Hot and sour	$ 4.00
Black bean	$ 4.00
French onion	$ 4.00
Wonton	$ 4.00
Vegetable	$ 4.00

Entrées

Hamburger	$ 8.95
Cheeseburger	$10.95
Fried chicken	$ 9.95
Filet of fish	$ 6.95
Chicken fajita	$ 8.95
Beef fajita	$10.95
Shrimp tempura	$10.95
Pork fried rice	$ 6.95
Steak au poivre	$12.95
Spaghetti and meatballs	$ 7.95
Chicken and hummus	$ 8.95
Lamb curry	$14.95

Vegetables & Side Dishes

Baked potato	$ 3.00
French fries	$ 3.00
Rice	$ 3.00
Corn on the cob (in season)	$ 3.00
Peas	$ 3.00
Green beans	$ 3.00
House salad	$ 4.50

Desserts

Homemade apple pie	$ 5.00
Chocolate mousse	$ 5.00
Flan	$ 5.00
Ice cream	$ 4.00
Mixed fresh fruit	$ 3.50

Drinks

Lemonade	$ 4.00
Coffee	$ 3.00
Tea	$ 3.00
Soda	$ 2.00

Credit cards accepted. No checks.

Unfortunately for Higgins, the competition was more intense than he had anticipated. After two months, his restaurant was doing poorly. One of his waitresses had quit and the number of customers was decreasing.

Prewriting

Work with a partner and brainstorm a list of solutions to Tom Higgins's problem.

SOLUTIONS

1. ______________________________
2. ______________________________
3. ______________________________
4. ______________________________
5. ______________________________
6. ______________________________

Writing

Use the list to plan and write an essay about solutions to Tom Higgins's problem. Choose several of the solutions on your list to develop into topics for the supporting paragraphs. Write an introduction that states the problem in a few sentences. End with a thesis statement that states the solutions you are going to discuss. Then write the supporting paragraphs using one solution for each paragraph. Finally, write a conclusion that leaves your reader thinking about the solutions.

Revising and Editing

Exchange drafts with a classmate. Discuss any suggestions that your partner has for revision and editing. Write or type a revised version of your essay.

Writing More Problem/Solution Essays

Follow these steps to write another problem/solution essay.

Prewriting

A. Choose one of the following topics and freewrite about it for 10 minutes. Use a separate piece of paper.

- Overcrowding in your school
- The generation gap
- An argument with a friend
- Smog
- Access to the workplace for the disabled

B. Using your freewriting as a basis for planning your essay, identify several of the solutions that you think you can develop into an essay. If you have not generated enough ideas, do another, more focused freewriting. Then prepare an outline of your essay.

Writing

On a separate piece of paper, write the first draft of your essay. Use the essay plan on page 19 to help you with your draft. Be sure to provide some background information on the problem in the introduction and include a clear thesis statement. Organize the supporting paragraphs according to order of importance, beginning or ending with the most important solution. End with a conclusion that summarizes the solutions, draws a conclusion, or makes a prediction.

Revising and Editing

A. Personal revising. Wait at least one day, and then revise your essay. Be sure that each paragraph describes one possible solution. Also, check to make sure you have provided enough support to explain each solution fully. Write or type a revised version of your essay.

B. Peer Revising. Exchange drafts with a classmate. Use the following worksheet as a guide for suggesting improvements in your partner's essay.

Writer: ____________________ Peer Editor: ____________________

1. What are some interesting things you learned from reading this essay?

____

____

____

2. Did the introduction provide enough background information to explain the problem? ____ yes ____ no

3. How many solutions did the author offer in the essay? ____________________

____

   Is each solution adequately developed in a separate supporting paragraph? ____ yes ____ no

4. Are the paragraphs arranged in a logical order? ____ yes ____ no

   What type of order did the author use? ____________________

5. Did the author use transitions to guide you from one idea to the next? ____ yes ____ no

6. Were there any irrelevant sentences that should be eliminated? ____ yes ____ no

7. Did the author include a conclusion that summarizes the solutions or makes a prediction? ____ yes ____ no

Incorporate any suggestions your classmate has made that you agree with.

C. Editing. Correct all the grammar, punctuation, capitalization, and spelling errors before you copy it over or type it.

Explore the Web

Think of a problem you might have in your everyday life: You spilled coffee on your carpet, you need directions to a nearby hospital, you want to buy an out-of-print book, you have a flat tire. Explore the Web to find a solution to your problem. Write a paragraph that describes the problem and explains the solution.

You Be the Editor

The following paragraph contains seven mistakes. Find the mistakes and correct them. Then copy the corrected paragraph onto a separate sheet of paper.

If you are like most people, you average one to three colds per year. Even if you do not have a cold right now. The chances are three in four that within the next year, at least one cold virus will find you. then you'll spend a week or so suffering from the miseries of the common cold: fatigue, sore throat, laryngitis, sneezing, stuffy or runny nose, and coughing. According to researchers, colds are the most common medical reason for missing school and work. Once you catch a cold, what can you do. There is no known cure yet for a cold. There are, however, several thing you can do to suppress the symptom's so that you feel better while the virus runs its course. For example, make sure that you get plenty of sleep and drink lots of liquids. You may find commercially available cold remedies such as decongestants, cough suppressants, and expectorants helpful, but keep in mind that these products can cause side effects. Many people prefer home remedies such as chicken soup, garlic, and ginger tea. In treating a cold, remember the wisdom of the ages, "if you treat a cold, it will be gone in a week; if you don't treat it, will be gone in seven days."

Source: *Jane Brody's Cold and Flu Fighter*

On Your Own

Write a problem/solution essay based on one of the problems you analyzed in the Brainstorming Solutions on pages 13–15. Be sure your essay has an introduction that describes the problem, several supporting paragraphs that explain the solutions, and a conclusion that summarizes the solutions or makes a prediction.

Unit 2

Business

Reading A: International Marketing *No Va*

Before You Read

You are going to read an article about advertising and marketing products in different countries.

Activate Your Background Knowledge

A. Read the statements in the chart. Do ycu agree or disagree with these statements? Check your response in the first two columns. You will check the last columns after you read.

Before You Read		Evaluate the Statements	After You Read	
Agree	Disagree	Statement	Agree	Disagree
		All products can be marketed the same way in different cultures.		
		Advertising slogans can always be translated successfully from one language to another.		
		International marketing is more successful when it appeals to each culture's particular values.		

B. Work with a partner. Discuss the statements and compare responses.

Preview and Predict

C. Read the title and subtitle of the article on pages 26–28. Look at the headings. Read the first and last paragraph of the article. Can you guess what the article will be about? Think of several topics that might be discussed in the article. Write the topics on the lines.

1. ____
2. ____
3. ____
4. ____

Preview the Vocabulary

D. The words in the box are boldfaced in the article. Use context clues to guess the meaning of the boldfaced words in the exercise. Write definitions or synonyms of the words. If necessary, use your dictionary. Then compare answers with a partner.

Words to Watch			
indicators	adaptations	shrinking	interpret
blunder	tricky	exaggeration	individualism
collectivism	slang	barrier	

1. Sometimes the cost of a product is an **indicator** of its quality. In fact, many people think that the more something costs, the better it is.

   ____

2. There were several **tricky** questions on the math test. It took me a long time to figure out the answers.

   ____

3. In some places forests are **shrinking**, while in other places deserts are getting bigger.

   ____

4. Some parts of the story were not appropriate for children, so I wrote an **adaptation** for a younger audience.

   ____

5. I made a terrible **blunder** when I called my professor by the wrong name. I hope he forgives me for my careless mistake.

   ____

6. John said that over a 1,000 people came to his concert last night. I'm sure the number is an **exaggeration**. There were probably more like 200 people in the audience.

   ____

7. In cultures where **individualism** is stressed, people believe in the value of personal success and independence.

   ____

8. On the other hand, in cultures where **collectivism** is stressed, people believe in the family, cooperation, and the importance of the group.

 ____

9. A chicken is a type of bird kept on a farm, but the word *chicken* is also **slang** for someone who isn't very brave.

 ____

10. Kim speaks Korean and José speaks Spanish. They are in the same English class and are becoming good friends despite their language **barrier**.

 ____

11. We **interpreted** his silence to mean that he was guilty.

 ____

Set a Purpose

You are going to read an article about international marketing. What do you want to find out about this topic? Write two questions you would like the article to answer.

1. ______________________________

2. ______________________________

As You Read

International Marketing *No Va*

How to Recognize Culture Differences and Sell a Product in a New Market

1 Your company is ready to take its new product to an international market. The product has sold well in Canada and there is a need for it in other countries. In addition, the economy is thriving. All the **indicators** are positive, so you use the same marketing campaign that worked in Canada. But you find that your early sales are much lower than you anticipated. Why? There are many possible reasons, but if history is any indication, one of the major failings of companies expanding to international markets is how they market the product, no matter how good it is.

2 You can't help but smile at the story of Chevrolet marketing their brand new Nova in Latin America in the early 1970s and then not understanding why it didn't sell. The problem lay in the language. *No va* in Spanish means "doesn't go," which is exactly what happened to the sales figures. To be fair to Chevrolet, they were not alone in their international marketing **blunder**. Gerber baby food, Coke, Pepsi, Perdue poultry, and Gillette have all taken their turn as the subject of international marketing jokes.

3 With modern technology **shrinking** our world, international borders are becoming less of a **barrier** between people. The temptation is to believe that this shrinkage will emphasize our cultural similarities when in fact the opposite has been found to be true. As companies become more global, many countries have become more protective of their culture. This increased sense of patriotism makes successful entry of foreign consumer products more difficult and the need for marketing **adaptations** more important.

4 In his best-selling book *The Lexus and the Olive Tree,* Thomas Friedman quotes his friend Yaron Ezrahi's observation about globalization. Ezrahi said: "There are two ways to make a person feel homeless—one is to destroy his home and the other is to make his home look and feel like everybody else's home." The best way to avoid creating a feeling of homelessness is to understand the culture you are selling to and make consumers think that your product is unique to their needs. Before you can understand marketing to new cultures, you must first understand what culture is. Culture can be defined as a set of values and beliefs that are learned, shared, and passed on to give us our identity. With that definition in mind, several cultural issues must be considered when marketing across cultures.

Be Careful When You Translate

5 Language is the most obvious concern you must think about when marketing across cultures. Translating the names of products and company names can be **tricky**. And you must be very careful when translating advertising slogans. When you decide to translate your company slogan or the name of the product, make sure that there are no **slang** expressions, which can lead to embarrassment. A notable and humorous example was the Chinese translation of Pepsi's slogan "Come alive with the Pepsi Generation," which translated to "Pepsi brings your ancestors back from the grave." This may have been good for sales, but I don't think Pepsi could actually do that.

Know the Meanings of Colors, Numbers, and Symbols

6 In different cultures, colors, numbers, and symbols have very different meanings. Know what the color of mourning is and don't advertise cars in that color. Learn what numbers are unlucky and avoid packaging items in those units. Understand which symbols do not transfer across cultures and then do not use them. For example, the thumbs-up sign may be a pleasant one in the United States, but Australians will **interpret** it very differently.

Consider Traditional Values

7 Cultures vary considerably in what they consider to be traditional values. For example, in Germany there is a tradition of excellence in engineering, in England, many people dislike **exaggeration**, and the Chinese have a tradition of valuing old, wise, and consistent over new, aggressive, and improved. Those traditions are only a few examples of the ones that must be known and considered for successful marketing.

Think about Individualism versus Collectivism

8 Another difference between cultures that should be considered is the importance placed on **individualism** versus **collectivism**. In the United States and Canada, individualism is very important. Many people in these countries believe in the value of personal success, independence, and the concept of "pulling yourself up by the boot straps" (solving a problem yourself without outside help). On the other hand, in collectivist cultures such as Japan, China, and Mexico, people believe in the family, cooperation, and the importance of the group. It is important to know whether the culture you are advertising to is individualistic or collectivistic; many mistakes can be made in not knowing. The central principle of marketing across cultures is no different from marketing within a single culture—know your market! The challenge is that it is easier to know about the culture you live in than one you are just visiting.

9 The most important thing is to know that there are cultural differences and to address them. Not all cultures are the same, and they don't want to be. Any effort to understand the differences will be well received and your balance sheet will provide you with proof.

After You Read

Check Your Comprehension

A. Circle the letter of the word or phrase that correctly completes each statement or answer the question.

1. The author believes that the successful entry of foreign products into a market is made more difficult because ________.
   a. many countries have become more protective of their culture
   b. cultural similarities are prevalent
   c. the quality of the products is poor
2. The term *culture* is defined in the ____________.
   a. first paragraph
   b. fourth paragraph
   c. last paragraph
3. Gerber baby food, Coke, Pepsi, Perdue poultry, and Gillette are used as examples of companies that ____________.
   a. have made a lot of money
   b. sell excellent products
   c. have made marketing blunders

4. According to the author, as our world is shrinking, many countries are becoming ______________.
   a. more protective of their culture
   b. less patriotic
   c. more individualistic
5. The thumbs-up sign is used as an example of ______________.
   a. an unlucky number
   b. a creative slogan
   c. a symbol that does not translate across cultures
6. Which culture has a tradition of valuing old, wise, and consistent over new, aggressive, and improved?
   a. Chinese
   b. Canadian
   c. German
7. The differences between individualistic and collectivist cultures are ______________.
   a. slightly significant
   b. very significant
   c. not significant
8. The author believes that the principle "know your market" is ______________.
   a. important both to marketing across cultures and within a single culture
   b. a collectivist point of view
   c. unimportant in today's shrinking world

Reading B

Levi's Gold

Dorothy Slate

[1]**Golden Gate** The entrance to San Francisco Bay in northern California from the Pacific Ocean.

[2]**Gold Rush** Gold was discovered in California in the late 1840s. As a result, many people rushed to California, hoping to find gold and become rich.

1 When the clipper ship sailed through California's Golden Gate[1] that March day in 1853, twenty-four-year-old Levi Strauss rushed to the deck, eager to see San Francisco. The Gold Rush[2], started in 1848, still drew men by the thousands to seek their fortunes. Strauss was one of them.

2 Six years earlier, he had left Bavaria in Germany to escape unfair laws against Jews and to join his older brothers Jonas and Louis in New York. They taught him English and told him peddling was an honorable occupation in the United States. Now he faced a new challenge. In his baggage were goods to sell. His brothers had helped select them in New York before he left on his long voyage around Cape Horn to California. Gold miners were sure to need thread, needles, scissors, thimbles, and rolls of canvas cloth for tents and wagon covers.

3 As Strauss looked toward the city, he saw several small boats approaching the ship. When they came close, some of their passengers clamored for news 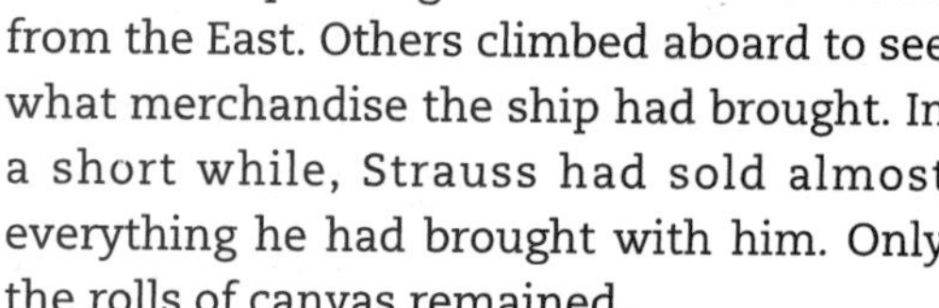 from the East. Others climbed aboard to see what merchandise the ship had brought. In a short while, Strauss had sold almost everything he had brought with him. Only the rolls of canvas remained.

4 Stepping ashore, he saw a bustling city with many "stores" that were merely tents or shanties. Among the ironworks, billiard-table manufacturers, dry-goods stores, breweries, and hundreds of saloons stood some stranded ships serving as hotels.

5 With gold dust from his sales aboard ship, Strauss bought a cart. He loaded his rolls of canvas and pushed the cart along wood-planked sidewalks. He parked on Montgomery Street, waiting for miners to pass by.

6 A prospector stopped to look at his canvas.

7 "It's for tenting," Strauss explained.

8 "Shoulda brought pants," the prospector told him. "Pants don't wear worth a hoot in the diggin's. Can't get a pair strong enough to last."

9 Instantly, the young entrepreneur sought out a tailor and created the first pair of jeans. Pleased with them, his customer later strutted around San Francisco. "Doggone, if a man ever had a pair of pants strong as Levi's before," he said.

10 The demand for "Levi's" grew so fast that Strauss could hardly keep up with it. When the brown canvas was gone, he switched to a sturdy fabric, *serge de Nîmes*, from Nîmes, France. The name was quickly shortened to "denim," and Strauss adopted the indigo blue familiar today.

11 Levi's brothers Jonas and Louis were his partners, as was David Stern, who had married Levi's sister Fanny. They decided to call their firm Levi Strauss & Company, agreeing that Levi was the "business head" in the family. Years went by, and the business grew.

12 Then, in July 1872, a letter arrived from Jacob W. Davis, a tailor in Reno. The letter explained that he was now reinforcing pants pocket corners with copper rivets. Rivets strengthened the seams, which tore out when miners and other workers stuffed their pockets with gold nuggets and tools.

13 Davis was flooded with orders but worried that someone would steal his idea. If Levi Strauss & Company would take out a patent in his name, Davis would give them half the right to sell the riveted clothing.

14 Strauss immediately saw the profit potential. Instead of nine or ten dollars a dozen, the riveted pants could bring thirty-six dollars just for adding a penny's worth of metal. It was a good risk.

15 The U.S. Patent Office took its time in granting Strauss a patent. It took ten months and many revisions and amendments before the Patent Office agreed that the idea of riveted pockets was unusual enough to be patented.

16 When Davis moved his family to San Francisco, Strauss put him in charge of production. Soon a force of sixty women stitched Levi's on a piecework basis. The orange thread still used today was an attempt to match the copper rivets. Another still-used trademark is the leather label featuring two teamsters whipping a pair of horses trying to tear apart the riveted pants.

17 Successful in business, Levi Strauss still found time to participate in many civic organizations and was well liked in San Francisco's business community. He never married, saying, "I am a bachelor, and I fancy on that account I need to work more, for my entire life is my business."

18 Although he had no children of his own, Strauss established many scholarships at the University of California, and when he died in 1902, he left money to Protestant, Catholic, and Jewish orphanages. He left the business to his sister Fanny's children.

19 Levi Strauss found gold not in streams or mines, but in fulfilling an everyday need. Today presidents, movie stars, and millions of other people wear Levi's and other brands of jeans, clothing created by an entrepreneur who responded to the needs of the market.

Identifying the Main Idea

Circle the letter of the statement that best expresses the main idea of the passage.

a. Gold miners bought Levi's pants because they were strong and durable.

b. Levi Strauss was able to make his fortune in jeans by responding to the needs of the market.

c. Levi was the "business head" of the Strauss family.

d. Levi Strauss was successful in business, but he still found time to participate in civic organizations.

Second Reading

Now reread "Levi's Gold" and do the exercises that follow.

How Well Did You Read?

Read the following statements. If a statement is true, write T *on the line. If it is false, write* F.

T 1. Levi's pants became popular very quickly.

____ 2. Levi brought canvas cloth to San Francisco to sell pants to the gold miners.

F 3. Levi Strauss & Co. was a family business.

T 4. The U.S. Patent Office quickly granted the patent for riveted pockets.

____ 5. Levi thought of using copper rivets to reinforce pocket corners.

Recalling Information

How Much Can You Remember?

Complete the paragraph with information from the article. See how much you can do without referring to the article. You do not have to use the exact words from the article as long as the idea is correct.

Levi Strauss went to ____________ in 1853 in search of ____________, but ended up making his fortune in ____________. He realized that a good way to make money was to make and sell ____________ ____________ that were suited for a ____________ lifestyle. His new business was very ____________, and soon many people were buying his ____________. In 1872, he made another good business decision; he added ____________ to his pant's pocket corners. This increased his ____________ even more. Today, jeans are as

_____ as ever. All types of people, including _____, _____, and even _____, can be seen wearing Levi jeans.

Organizing Information

Here is a list of important events in Levi Strauss's life. Put them in correct time order by numbering them from 1 to 7.

_____ a. Levi sold his first pair of pants.
_____ b. Levi left Germany to join his brothers in New York.
_____ c. He got a patent for riveted pockets.
_____ d. He moved to San Francisco.
_____ e. He began using blue denim to make his pants.
_____ f. Levi Strauss & Company was established.
_____ g. He left his business to his sister's children.

Figure It Out

Vocabulary in Context

Without using your dictionary, write an approximate definition or a synonym for the highlighted words in the following sentences. Then compare your answers with those of your classmates.

1. The Gold Rush, started in 1848, still **drew** men by the thousands to seek their fortunes.

_____

_____

2. Pleased with [his pants], his customer later **strutted** around San Francisco.

_____

_____

3. The demand for "Levi's" grew so fast that Strauss could hardly **keep up** with it.

_____

_____

4. When the brown canvas was gone, he **switched** to a sturdy fabric, *serge de Nîmes*, from Nîmes, France.

_____

_____

5. Rivets strengthened the seams, which tore out when miners and other workers **stuffed** their pockets with gold nuggets and tools.

____

____

6. Davis was **flooded** with orders but worried that someone would steal his idea.

____

____

7. Today presidents, movie stars, and millions of other people wear Levis and other **brands** of jeans.

____

Talk It Over

Discussion Questions

1. Levi Strauss sold his first pair of pants in 1853. Today his idea for practical pants is still influencing the fashion world. Why do you think jeans are still so popular?
2. In the last paragraph the author states, "Levi Strauss found gold not in streams or mines, but in fulfilling an everyday need." What was the need that he fulfilled? What do you think made him such a successful entrepreneur? What are the qualities that make someone successful in business?

Reading C

Our sense of smell can influence our behavior in many ways. Decisions about what we eat, what we wear, who we are attracted to, and even what we buy can be influenced by smell. In Smells Sell!, *you will read about how advertisers use the sense of smell to increase sales.*

Before You Read

Making Predictions

1. Read the title, subtitle, and headings of this article. Also, look at the picture. What do you think the article will be about? Write your prediction on the lines provided.

____

____

____

2. Now read the first and last two paragraphs of the article. Can you make your prediction more specific?

___

___

___

3. Finally, read the first sentence of each paragraph. Do you want to change your prediction at all? If so, write your new prediction below.

___

___

___

Reading the Article

Now read the whole article, and do the exercises that follow.

Reading C

Smells Sell!

Melinda Crow

Scent Experts Lead You by the Nose

1 You're standing in the cereal aisle at the grocery store, searching for your favorite brand. Suddenly, you catch a whiff of chocolate-chip cookies. Your mouth begins to water. You forget about cereal and head for the bakery section.

2 Guess what? You just walked into a trap—an odor trap! The yummy smell was fake. The odor was cooked up by scientists in a lab, then spread by the store's owners to lure you to the bakery section.

DOLLARS AND SCENTS

3 For years, scientists have been studying the special powers of smells. It seems that our noses and our brains are very closely connected. When you smell something, the odor goes up your nose to smelling zones. From here, sense cells send nerve messages to your brain telling it what you smelled.

4 More than our other four senses, our sense of smell changes our mood and helps us remember things. If you were told to think about popcorn, you'd probably recall its smell. And then you might remember the movie you saw while eating it. Our sense of smell also helps us sniff out danger—like the smell of smoke. And it can make your mouth water from just one whiff of food.

5 If smell is so powerful, say store owners, then maybe it can also sell products. So businesses have begun spending thousands of dollars to scent entire stores. Fake scents are being used to lead customers by the nose. These bogus odors help to get people inside and put them in the mood to buy. They even make customers remember the store later, so they'll come back for more.

6 Some business people predict that in 10 years, store smells will be as common as the soft music stores often play to put shoppers in a good mood.

HIDDEN PELLETS AND GOO

7 J'Amy Owens designs stores for a living. To keep up with the new trend in store odors, she recently began including "fragrance planning" as part of her store design. She believes each store should have its own special smell.

8 For a kids' clothing store in San Francisco, CA, for example, she's using the smell of cinnamon and hot apple spice. She hopes shoppers will end up thinking these kids' clothes are as American as apple pie!

9 Sometimes Owens gets strange requests. "The owner of a fast-food restaurant wanted to know if I could scent the speaker at the drive-up window," she says.

10 Owens spreads the store scents secretly, using little balls soaked in fragrance. She hides them in light fixtures and heating pipes. If that doesn't give off enough odor, she puts in a small heater. This warms up the fragrance. A fan then spreads this smell throughout the store.

11 Other stores use computer-controlled machines to carry the smell out through the store's air vents. Getting the right amount of odor in the air can be tricky. When Steven Schultz first started using peach fragrance in his discount store in Louisville, KY, the whole place ended up smelling like a peach warehouse.

SOMETHING SMELLS FISHY

12 Dr. Alan Hirsch designs smells for businesses. He says that it doesn't take a whole lot of smell to affect you. Store owners can lure you to the candy aisle—even if you don't realize you're smelling candy. This idea scares a lot of people. Groups that protect the rights of shoppers are upset. They say the stores are using a kind of brainwashing, which they call "smellwashing."

13 "It's pretty sleazy," says Mark Silbergeld. He runs an organization that checks out products for consumers.

14 The scientists hired to design the scents disagree. "There's mellow background music, there's neon lighting, there are all sorts of bells and jingles being used," says Dr. Hirsch. "Why not smells?"

15 One reason why not, says Silbergeld, is that some people are allergic to certain scents pumped into products or stores.

16 But there's a whole other side to this debate. Do the smells really work? So far there is little proof one way or the other. But Dr. Hirsch has run some interesting experiments.

17 In one of Hirsch's experiments, 31 volunteers were led into a sneaker store that smelled slightly like flowers. Later, another group shopped in the same store, but with no flower odor.

18 Dr. Hirsch found that 84 percent of the shoppers were more likely to buy the sneakers in the flower-scented room. But Hirsch found out something even stranger.

19 "Whether the volunteers liked the flower scent or not didn't matter," Hirsch says. "Some reported that they hated the smell. But they still were more likely to buy the shoes in the scented room."

WHO KNOWS THE FUTURE?

20 Using smells to sell products isn't new. In 1966, a company added lemon fragrance to its dish detergent. They wanted people to think the soap contained "natural" cleaners. It worked! Today, businesses spend over a billion dollars a year just on product odor.

21 Some companies have already discovered ways to make microwaveable foods smell good before they're cooked. They scent the packages. Smell for yourself. Next time you pop a bag of microwave popcorn, smell the bag before you put it in the microwave. Chances are, it already smells like popped corn.

22 New uses for smells are being created every day. One bank, for example, gives customers coupons advertising car loans. To get people to take out a loan, bank officials hope to coat these coupons with the fresh leather smell of a new car.

23 In Australia, companies are putting sweat odor on unpaid bills. Since some people sweat when they're scared, this smell might remind them of when they are frightened. And they'll pay the bills right away.

24 What lies ahead for our noses? Smell scientists are working on some outrageous ideas. Would you believe TV sets that produce smells? Or how about odor diets? Certain food smells will fool your stomach into thinking it's full.

25 Alarm clocks will scent your bedroom with an aroma designed to wake you up. Scientists are even working on ways to keep garbage from stinking. And researchers expect scents to one day help students make more sense of what they're learning.

How Well Did You Read?

True/False

Read the statements that follow. If a statement is true, write T *on the line. If it is false, write* F.

_____ 1. The sense of smell can change your mood and help you remember things.

_____ 2. Because the sense of smell is so powerful, some businesses have begun using it to sell products.

_____ 3. In the future, store smells might be as common as soft music.

_____ 4. It takes a large amount of a certain smell to affect a customer.

_____ 5. It is always easy to get the right amount of odor in the air.

_____ 6. Some groups and organizations oppose the idea of using smells to attract and influence customers.

_____ 7. There is a lot of evidence supporting the idea that smells influence customer behavior.

_____ 8. Using smells to sell products is a new development in marketing.

_____ 9. New uses for smells are being developed all the time.

Supporting Main Ideas

Using Examples

Find examples in the article to support each of the following ideas.

1. More than our other four senses, our sense of smell changes our mood and helps us remember things.

   ____

   ____

2. Each store should have its own special smell.

   ____

   ____

3. Getting the right amount of odor in the air can be tricky.

   ____

   ____

4. Using smells to sell products isn't new.

   ____

   ____

5. Some companies have already discovered ways to make microwaveable foods smell good before they're cooked.

   ____

   ____

6. New uses for smells are being created every day.

   ____

   ____

Figure It Out

Idioms And Expressions

An **idiom** is a phrase that has a special meaning. The meaning of the phrase as a whole is different from the meanings of the individual words in the phrase. For example, in the sentence, "I'm sure David was pulling my leg when he told me he had won the lottery," the idiom *pulling my leg* means teasing me.

An **expression** is also a group of words with a special meaning. For example, in the sentence, "She hopes shoppers will end up thinking these kids' clothes are as American as apple pie," the expression *as American as apple pie* means that something is very American.

"Smells Sell!" is filled with idioms and expressions. Circle the letter of the word or phrase that best describes the idiom.

1. You forget about cereal and **head for** the bakery section.
   a. walk toward
   b. point your head at
   c. remember
2. You just **walked into a trap**—an odor trap!
   a. avoided
   b. got tricked
   c. smelled
3. The odor was **cooked up** by scientists in a lab....
   a. sold
   b. invented
   c. discussed
4. Fake scents are being used **to lead customers by the nose.**
   a. direct customers
   b. get rid of customers
   c. discourage customers
5. He runs an organization that **checks out** products for customers.
   a. removes
   b. leaves
   c. investigates
6. But Hirsch **found out** something even stranger.
   a. wrote about
   b. discovered
   c. examined

Talk It Over

Discussion Questions

1. Consider again how sensitive you are to smells. Do you think it's realistic to think that artificial smells can influence your buying behavior?
2. "Synthetic fragrances just add more chemicals to the chemical soup. It's an outrage." (Dr. Albert Robbins, environmental medicine specialist[1]) What do you think Dr. Robbins means? Do you think indoor air pollution is a major health risk?
3. Do you use incense, cologne, aftershave lotion, perfume, or potpourri? Which ones? Do you use them often?

[1]The Environmental Magazine (July/August 1993), 10.

Unit Three

Comparison/Contrast

Section I: Reading

Harry Potter and *The Lord of the Rings*

Before You Read

Work in small groups. Discuss these questions.

1. What kind of movies do you enjoy watching? Action movies? Romantic comedies? Horror movies?
2. What was the last really good movie you saw at the theater? What was it about, and why was it so good?

3. Make a list of movies your group would recommend to other students. Explain why you think other people would enjoy each movie. When you have finished, share your answers with the class.

In a movie review, a movie critic writes a short summary of the story and gives his or her opinion about the movie. Critics often award stars to show how good a movie is. Five stars means excellent; one, or even no stars, means you're better off staying at home! Look at the title of the reading on pages 44 and 45. How many stars do you think these two movies will get?

Using Context Clues to Understand Vocabulary

Read the sentence pairs. The words in bold print in the first sentence are in the reading on pages 44–45. Underline the word or words in the second sentence that are similar in meaning to those in bold print

1. Last week I saw a really **depressing** movie about a young girl who went to the city to find work, but ended up homeless because no one would employ her. It made me feel sad.

   depressing: ______________________________

2. In the movie *Gandhi*, Ben Kingsley **portrays** Mohandas Gandhi brilliantly. He looks, speaks, and moves just like him.

   portrays: ______________________________

3. Harry Potter **fans** waited for hours until the fourth book in the series was released. People who admire these books even waited in the pouring rain for their copy.

   fans: ______________________________

4. **Special effects** are created using computer technology. Sometimes what you see on the screen looks so real you forget it is a computer-generated image.

   special effects: ______________________________

5. The battle scene in the movie *The Patriot* was very **convincing**. At one point, the action was so lifelike I jumped out from my seat to avoid a sword-waving soldier.

   convincing: ______________________________

Now Read

Harry Potter and the Sorcerer's Stone and *The Lord of the Rings: The Fellowship of the Ring*

1 Last weekend was cold, wet, and miserable, even depressing. I decided to make the best of this gloomy weather by watching two of my favorite movies from my collection. These movies chased the clouds away and turned the gray rain into dazzling sunlight. My sixteen-year-old son agreed after watching the movies with me, "They are brilliant, Dad!" I guarantee you will think so, too. *Harry Potter and the Sorcerer's Stone* and *Lord of the Rings: The Fellowship of the Ring* will go down in history as two of the best movies from the first decade of the twenty-first century. It's worth seeing them for a second time.

2 The movies share striking similarities. First of all, both come from extremely popular novels which have sold millions of copies worldwide. Devoted fans of these books looked forward to the movie versions with some nervousness. Would the movies be as good as the books? Would the actors portray the characters as magically as they are portrayed in the written print? As a fan of J. K. Rowling's Harry Potter books, and having grown up reading J. R. R. Tolkien's *The Lord of the Rings*, my answer is a resounding yes! The movies were as good as the books.

3 The movies also have similar themes: the battle of good against evil, the power of friendship, and the power of individual courage. Harry Potter is an orphan who is living with his mean aunt and uncle. On his eleventh birthday, he finds out what his relatives have known all along. He is a wizard, and a very special one at that. With the help of a giant named Hagrid, Harry travels to Hogwarts School of Witchcraft and Wizardry, where he meets two friends, Hermione and Ron. There he fights the evil Voldemort, who is trying to regain power. Likewise, in *The Lord of the Rings*, young Frodo, accompanied by friends Sam and Aragorn, must return a magical ring before it is stolen by the evil Saruman. The twists and turns of these tales will keep you guessing—even if you have read the books!

4 The special effects in both movies are masterful. In the Quidditch scene, Harry seems to soar through the theater right at the audience. Similarly, the scene where the three friends battle with "real" chess pieces will have you gripping the edge of your seat. In *The Lord of the Rings*, the special effects are perhaps even more amazing. Huge armies of terrifying monsters thunder across the screen, leaving you to wonder how on earth Frodo is going to succeed. These movies can easily stand side by side with *Star Wars* and *Jurassic Park* in terms of special effects.

5 The final similarity is the quality of acting. Chris Columbus, director of *Harry Potter*, and Peter Jackson, director of *Lord of the Rings*, chose a combination of brilliant, well-known actors and new faces. Richard Harris plays Professor Dumbledore in *Harry Potter* as masterfully as Sir Ian McKellen portrays Gandalf. Maggie Smith is amazing as Professor McGonagall in *Harry Potter*, and Cate Blanchett is a magical Galadriel. A new actor, Daniel Radcliffe, is a convincing Harry, although perhaps he is a little overshadowed by the remarkable performance of another new face—Rupert Grint as Ron. In *Lord of the Rings*, the little known Elijah Wood plays Frodo in a charming and innocent way which makes his bravery all the more remarkable.

6 Good books live forever; good movies live almost as long. Viewers will enjoy these movies over and over again. I'm looking forward to the next spell of depressing weather when I will sit down and watch two more memorable movies. Meanwhile, to *Harry Potter* and *Lord of the Rings,* I award the following:

Harry Potter and the Sorcerer's Stone * * * * 1/2

Lord of the Rings: The Fellowship of the Ring * * * * *

Both movies are rated PG-13. Go see them. You won't be disappointed.

After You Read

How Well Did You Read?

Work in small groups. Read the statements. Write T *(true),* F *(false), or* N *(not enough information). Underline the information from the reading that supports your answer.*

_____ 1. The author thinks both are excellent movies.

_____ 2. Harry and Frodo are both orphans who fight against evil.

_____ 3. People who have read the books will not enjoy these movies.

_____ 4. According to the reviewer, the special effects in these movies are outdated.

_____ 5. These movies have similar themes.

Check Your Understanding

A. Work in small groups. Discuss the questions, and share your answers with the class.

1. According to the reading, in what ways are these movies similar?
2. Do you agree that sometimes a book is better than a movie? Explain your answer.
3. The reviewer points out that both movies are about the theme of good against evil. Can you think of any other books or movies that are also about this theme? List the titles of these books or movies:

    a. ______________________________

    b. ______________________________

    c. ______________________________

B. Read each question and circle the letter of the best answer.

1. How is most of this reading organized?
    a. time order
    b. comparison
    c. contrast
2. In the first paragraph, why does the reviewer say he was depressed?
    a. The weather was bad.
    b. An old movie made him feel that way.
    c. *Harry Potter and the Sorcerer's Stone* made him sad.

3. In paragraph 1, how does the writer communicate his son's opinion of the movies?
   a. by using a direct quotation
   b. by using an indirect quotation
   c. by using both a direct quotation and an indirect quotation
4. Why were fans of the books nervous about seeing these movies?
   a. They thought the movies would be better than the books.
   b. They worried that the movies would not be as good as the books.
   c. They worried that the movies would not be made.
5. When did the critic read *The Lord of the Rings* for the first time?
   a. just before he watched the movie
   b. when he became a movie critic
   c. when he was a child
6. Who represents "good" in these two movies?
   a. Harry, Hermione, and Ron
   b. Gandalf and Voldemort
   c. Harry and Frodo
7. In paragraph 3, what does the transition *likewise* introduce?
   a. an additional example
   b. a similar example
   c. a contrasting example
8. What does the writer think of the special effects in these two movies?
   a. They are better than *Star Wars* and *Jurassic Park*.
   b. They are not as good as *Star Wars* and *Jurassic Park*.
   c. They are the same quality as *Star Wars* and *Jurassic Park*.
9. Which statement is correct according to the reading?
   a. Richard Harris is a better actor than Sir Ian McKellen.
   b. Rupert Grint gave a better performance than Daniel Radcliffe.
   c. Elijah Wood was not very convincing as Frodo.
10. Why is this critic "almost looking forward to the next spell of depressing weather"?
   a. Because he will be able to watch *Harry Potter* and *Lord of the Rings* again.
   b. Because he will have time to watch two different movies.
   c. Because he likes the rain.

Reading Skill

Recognizing Similarities

The Previous reading **compares,** or looks for similarities between, two movies. Writers use signals to introduce comparisons. These signals include:

like both likewise similarly as _____ as

Examples *Like* Frodo, Harry is a young boy who has to fight evil.

Both authors of these novels are British.

Harry is helped by two friends—Hermione and Ron. *Likewise* (or *similarly*), Frodo is helped by Sam and Aragorn.

The movies are *as* good *as* the books.

Recognizing these signals helps you to understand the reading more easily.

A. Reread the article on pages 44–45. Underline the words that signal comparisons.

B. Now, using the underlined words to help you, complete the following chart showing the comparisons from the reading.

	The Sorcerer's Stone	**The Fellowship of the Ring**
Represents good:		*Frodo*
Represents evil:		
Loyal, trustworthy friends:	*Ron and Hermione*	
Scenes with excellent special effects:		
Well-known actors:		
New, less-known actors:		
Rated:		
Authors of original books:		

Vocabulary Skill

Recognizing Expressions

In English, many words are often used together as a phrase or an **expression**. In order to understand an expression, you need to use context clues from the sentences around the expression. It is not helpful to translate each separate word.

For example,

I ***made the most of*** *this gloomy weather by previewing two movies which chased the clouds away and turned the gray rain into dazzling sunlight.*

To make the most of something: to take advantage of a situation that is not perfect.

Reading/Writing—Fielding

Reading is an excellent way to build your knowledge of expressions. You should remember expressions as phrases rather than individual words.

A. The following expressions are in the reading on pages 44–45. Scan the reading to locate them. Use context clues and match the expression with the correct definition.

_____	1. go down in history as	a. to be of equal quality
_____	2. twists and turns	b. full of excitement or fear
_____	3. gripping the edge of your seat	c. be remembered as
_____	4. stand side by side with	d. rapidly changing story

B. Now complete the sentences in your own words.

1. The Columbia shuttle disaster in 2003 will go down in history as_______________

   ____.

2. There were so many twists and turns to the story that I _______________

   ____.

3. I found myself gripping the edge of the seat because _______________

   ____.

4. In my opinion, *Star Wars: Episode II—Attack of the Clones* cannot stand side by side with the first *Star Wars* movie. The first movie was _______________

   ____.

Life Skill

Understanding Rating Systems

Parents want to make sure that their children are watching appropriate (suitable) movies at the theater and on TV. They also want their children to play appropriate video games. To help parents decide which movies or games are suitable for their children, many countries have rating systems. Parents can look for a clear icon, or symbol, that indicates the age suitability for the movie or the game. For example, a film that is rated G, for general audiences, is appropriate for children of all ages.

A. Read these ratings out loud with a partner. If you don't understand a word, try to guess its meaning. If you can't guess, look it up in an English dictionary.

MOVIES

G **GENERAL AUDIENCES**
All Ages Admitted

PG **PARENTAL GUIDANCE SUGGESTED**
Some Material May Not Be Suitable For Children

PG-13 **PARENTS STRONGLY CAUTIONED**
Some Material May Be Inappropriate for Children Under 13

R **RESTRICTED**
UNDER 17 REQUIRES ACCOMPANYING PARENT OR ADULT GUARDIAN

NC-17 NO ONE 17 AND UNDER ADMITTED

VIDEO GAMES

eC Content may be suitable for ages 3 and older. Contains no material that parents would find inappropriate.

E Content suitable for ages 6 and older.

T Content may be suitable for persons 13 and older. May contain violent content, mild or strong language, and/or suggestive themes.

M Content may be suitable for people 17 and older. May contain mature themes or more intense violence.

A Adults only. Not intended for persons under 18.

RP Rating pending.

B. Work with a partner. Answer the questions in complete sentences. When you have finished, share your answers with the class.

1. Do you think rating systems successfully protect children from playing or seeing inappropriate games and movies? Explain your answer.

____

____

____

2. In your country, what happens if two fifteen-year-olds try to get into a movie intended for an adult audience?

____

____

____

____

3. Imagine that your favorite TV show is a movie. What movie rating would you give it? Explain your answer and give reasons.

____

____

____

____

Unit Three Above material from: *Read Ahead 2*

Section II: Writing

Very often in your writing, you will want to show how ideas, people, or things are similar or different. In these cases, you will use a **comparison/contrast** type of essay. When you **compare** two things, you look for how they are similar. When you **contrast** two things, you look for how they are different. It is important that the two things you compare or contrast belong to the same general class. For example, you probably would not want to compare or contrast a house and a dog. You could, however, compare and contrast a Japanese house and a North American house.

In academic writing, comparison and contrast are often used to support a point or persuade the reader. For example, in a political science class, you might compare and contrast two leaders in order to prove which one was more successful at bringing about economic reforms. In a literature class, you might compare and contrast two short stories to show which one you liked better. In an engineering class, you might compare and contrast two methods of combustion to explain why one is more efficient than the other.

The Language of Comparison and Contrast: Useful Phrases and Sentence Patterns

COMPARISON

and . . . too	Tokyo has an efficient subway system, **and** London does **too.**
as . . . as	Tokyo's subway system is **as** efficient **as** London's.
likewise	Tokyo has an efficient subway system. **Likewise**, London has an efficient subway system.
similarly	Tokyo has an efficient subway system. **Similarly**, London has an efficient subway system.
alike	New York City and Tokyo are **alike** in several ways.
both . . . and	**Both** Japan **and** Korea are in Asia.
like	The weather in Philadelphia is **like** the weather in Istanbul.
similar to	The population of Vienna is **similar to** the population of Frankfurt.
the same	Philadelphia has **the same** kind of weather as Istanbul.
the same as	The altitude of Calcutta is **the same as** the altitude of Copenhagen.

CONTRAST

but	The Sahara desert has a dry climate, **but** the Amazon rain forest has a wet climate.
different from	The climate in the Sahara desert is very **different from** the climate in the Amazon rain forest.
however	The Sahara desert has a dry climate. **However**, the Amazon rain forest has a wet climate.
in contrast	The Sahara desert has a dry climate. **In contrast**, the Amazon rain forest has a wet climate.
on the other hand	The Sahara desert has a dry climate. **On the other hand**, the Amazon rain forest has a wet climate.
while	**While** the Sahara desert is dry, the Amazon rain forest is wet.
whereas	**Whereas** the Sahara desert is dry, the Amazon rain forest is wet.
unlike	**Unlike** rain forests, deserts get very little rain.
although	**Although** the Sahara desert has a dry climate, some crops can be grown there.
even though	**Even though** the Sahara desert has a dry climate, some crops can be grown there.

The following sentence patterns are useful in writing topic sentences and thesis statements for comparison/contrast essays and paragraphs:

1. **There are several** | differences / similarities | **between** ____ **and** ____.

There are several *differences* ***between*** *high school* ***and*** *college.*

There are several *similarities* ***between*** *high school* ***and*** *college.*

2. ____ **and** ____ **are** | similar / different | **in many ways.**

Thai food ***and*** *Vietnamese food* ***are*** *similar* ***in many ways.***

Thai food ***and*** *Vietnamese food* ***are*** *different* ***in many ways.***

3. ____ **is** | different from / similar to | ____ **in many ways.**

My father ***is*** *different from his older brother* ***in many ways.***

My father ***is*** *similar to his older brother* ***in many ways.***

4. ____ **and** ____ **have** | several / many | **things in common.**

My best friend ***and*** *I* ***have*** *several* ***things in common.***

5. **A comparison between** ____ **and** ____ | reveals / shows / demonstrates | ____.

A comparison between *jazz* ***and*** *rock 'n' roll reveals some surprising similarities.*

A comparison between *jazz* ***and*** *rock 'n' roll reveals some surprising differences.*

Write a sample thesis statement for a comparison/contrast essay on each of the following topics. Use a variety of the sentence patterns modeled above.

1. Topic: Chinese food and Mexican food

   Thesis statement: ____________________

2. Topic: Soccer and basketball

   Thesis statement: ____________________

3. Topic: Capitalism and communism

   Thesis statement: ____________________

4. Topic: American cars and Japanese cars

   Thesis statement: ____________________

5. Topic: Two of your classmates

   Thesis statement: ______________________________

Examining Comparisons and Contrasts

Look at the following two classified ads for apartments for rent. Find several similarities and differences between the two apartments. Write two sentences of comparison and two sentences of contrast.

1.

Apartments for Rent

Large 2-bedroom apt., 2 bathrooms, eat-in kitchen, large living room, air-conditioning, wall-to-wall carpeting, great location on Monument Street, NO pets, $700/month, all utilities included. Call Mr. Toll at (315) 446–3377.	**Huron Towers:** 10th floor—great view of river, **3 bedrooms,** 2 bathrooms, modern kitchen with new appliances, fireplace in living room, hardwood floors, air-conditioning, laundry facilities, utilities NOT included. NO pets. Pool and tennis courts on premises. $995/month. Call for appointment: (315) 885–3909.

Example

a. *The apartment on Monument Street has fewer bedrooms than the apartment in Huron Towers.*

b. ______________________________

c. ______________________________

d. ______________________________

Now do the same for the next two sets of classified ads.

2.

Used Cars for Sale

2001 Toyota Camry. Automatic transmission. Excellent condition. Fully loaded. 18,000 miles. Gray leather interior, dark green exterior. ABS brakes. Sun roof. Driver's side air bag. CD player. $21,000. Call (413) 248–5573.	**2000 Audi Quattro.** Mint condition. Standard transmission. 25,000 miles. Loaded. Silver with black leather interior. Sun roof. ABS brakes. Seat heaters. Tape deck. Dual air bags. Theft alarm system. $28,000. Call (508) 427–0511.

____

a. ______________________________

b. ______________________________

c. ______________________________

d. ______________________________

3.

PETS

Golden Retriever puppy for sale. 5-month-old male. Great with kids. One-year health guarantee. $100. Call (617) 368–3254.	**German Shepherd puppy** needs home. Female, 7 months. House-trained. Excellent watch dog. Health guarantee for first year. $100. Call (617) 576–3124 after 6 P.M.

a. ______________________________

b. ______________________________

c. ______________________________

d. ______________________________

Writing about Comparisons

You are studying the impact of heredity on human behavior and are doing research on identical twins who were separated at birth. The paragraph below is the introductory paragraph you have written for your report.

> Some of the most important research in the field of behavioral genetics comes from the studies of identical twins who were separated at birth. Dr. Thomas J. Bouchard is a professor at the University of Minnesota who has conducted many influential studies on identical twins. He believes that by examining their differences and similarities, we will better understand the mysteries of heredity and environment. One of the most revealing pair of twins that Dr. Bouchard has studied is known as "the Jim twins." Jim Springer and Jim Lewis are identical twins who were separated at birth because their 14-year-old mother could not take care of them. They were not reunited until 39 years later. According to Dr. Bouchard, the Jim twins are "the most valuable pair that has ever been studied" because the similarities between them are so astounding.
>
> Source: *Good Housekeeping*

On a separate piece of paper, write a paragraph on the similarities between Jim Springer and Jim Lewis. The following is a list of the similarities that you have gathered. There are too many similarities listed here for one paragraph. Choose the ones that you think are the most interesting to include in your paragraph. Remember to begin your paragraph with a clearly stated topic sentence.

- Each brother was told that his brother had died at birth.
- Both brothers are emotional, sentimental, kind, generous, friendly, and loving by nature.
- Neither brother gets angry easily, and if he does get angry, he doesn't show it.
- Both bite their fingernails and/or jiggle one foot when nervous.
- They look exactly alike.
- They are both 6 feet tall and weigh 180 pounds.
- They walk the same way.
- Both cross their legs the same way.

- Their voices sound exactly the same.
- They use the same gestures when they speak.
- Both use the same expressions, such as "Mama mía" and "Cool."
- Both enjoy woodworking and have built several birdhouses and tables.
- Both brothers are poor spellers.
- Both were married first to women named Linda.
- Their second wives were both named Betty.
- As children, they each had a dog and named it Toy.
- They have both taken family vacations on the same beach in Florida.
- Until they were reunited, each had felt an emptiness, as though something was missing from his life.
- Jim Springer named his son James Allen; Jim Lewis named his son James Alan.
- Both frequently buy gifts (that they cannot afford) for their wives.
- Both men have worked part time in law enforcement.

Now revise and edit your paragraph. Copy it over and give it to your teacher.

Methods of Organization for Comparison and Contrast

There are two basic patterns for writing a comparison/contrast essay: the **block method** and the **point-by-point method**.

In the block method, you describe all the similarities in the first supporting paragraph and then all the differences in the second supporting paragraph.

In the point-by-point method, you identify several important points to be compared and contrasted. In the first supporting paragraph, you compare and contrast the two things according to the first point. In the second supporting paragraph, you compare and contrast the two things according to the second point, and so on. Most student writers find the block method easier to master.

The following 2 essays on pages 56–58 demonstrate these styles.

Analyzing Essays of Comparison and Contrast

Read the following two essays. The purpose of both essays is to explain why a student chose to attend Greenwell University rather than State University.

ESSAY 1

Last week when I received acceptances from my top two choices for college, State and Greenwell, I knew I had a difficult decision to make. Although I had talked to friends and relatives who had attended both schools and had visited both campuses many times, I couldn't make up my mind. It was only after I analyzed the similarities and differences between the two schools that I finally came to my decision to begin classes at Greenwell in the fall.

At first glance, it seems that State and Greenwell have a lot in common. First of all, both universities are located in Pennsylvania, where I am from. The tuition is also exactly the same at both schools—$20,000 per year. In addition, the basketball team at State is just as good as the one at Greenwell, and I would love to play for either one. Most importantly, both schools have large libraries, excellent academic reputations, and first-class engineering departments.

It was when I looked at the differences between the two schools that I made my final decision. In terms of location, State is more attractive. Its setting in a safe suburb was definitely more appealing than Greenwell's location in a dangerous city neighborhood. I also liked State's older campus with its beautiful buildings and trees more than Greenwell's new campus, which looks like an office complex. But I realized that these should not be the most important factors in my decision. I had to pay a lot of attention to the financial component. Although the tuition is the same at both schools, Greenwell offered me a $3,000 scholarship, whereas State couldn't give me any financial aid. In addition, if I go to Greenwell, I can live at home and save money on room and board. Since Greenwell is much closer to home, I won't have to spend as much on transportation to and from school. The most important factor in making my decision was the difference in class size between the two universities. State has large classes and an impersonal feeling. On the other hand, Greenwell has small classes, and students get a lot of personal attention.

In conclusion, after taking everything into consideration, I think I made the right decision. Since small classes, personal attention from my professors, and saving money are all very important to me, I will probably be happier at Greenwell.

Work with a Partner

Answer the following questions with a partner.

1. What method did the author of this essay use?

   ____

2. What is the thesis statement?

   ____

3. What is the topic sentence of the first supporting paragraph?

   ____

4. What similarities between the two schools does the author mention?

   ____

   ____

   ____

   ____

5. What is the topic sentence of the second supporting paragraph?

   ____

6. What differences between the two schools does the author mention?

   ____

   ____

   ____

   ____

ESSAY 2

Last week when I received acceptances from my top two choices for college, State and Greenwell, I knew I had a difficult decision to make. Although I had talked to friends and relatives who had attended both schools and had visited both campuses many times, I couldn't make up my mind. It was only after I compared the location, cost, and quality of education of the two schools that I could finally come to my decision to attend Greenwell.

The first thing I considered was the location. First of all, both universities are located in Pennsylvania, where I am from. But that is where the similarities end. State's setting in a safe suburb is definitely more appealing than Greenwell's location in a dangerous city neighborhood. I also like State's older campus with its beautiful buildings and gardens more than Greenwell's new campus, which looks like an office complex.

In addition to location, I had to pay a lot of attention to the financial component. The tuition is the same at both schools—$20,000 per year. However, Greenwell offered me a $3,000 scholarship, but State couldn't give me any money. Also, if I go to Greenwell, I can live at home and save money on room and board. Finally, since Greenwell is much closer to home, I won't have to spend as much on transportation to and from school.

The quality of education at the two schools had the most influence on my decision. In many ways, State and Greenwell have similar standards of education. Both schools have large libraries and excellent academic reputations. Also, State has a first-class engineering department, and so does Greenwell. So I had to look at other things. What it came down to was the difference in class size between the two universities. State has large classes and an impersonal feeling. On the other hand, Greenwell has small classes, and students get a lot of personal attention.

In conclusion, after taking everything into consideration, I think I made the right decision. Since small classes, saving money, and personal attention from my professors are very important to me, I will probably be happier at Greenwell.

Work with a Partner

Answer the following questions with a partner.

1. What method did the author of this essay use?

   ____

2. What is the thesis statement?

   ____

3. What three points about the schools did the author compare and contrast?

   ____

   ____

   ____

4. How did the author organize the order of the supporting paragraphs within the essay? Least important to most important? Or most important to least important?

   ____

5. What transitions did the author use to connect the ideas in the essay? Underline them.

Essay Plans: Comparison/Contrast

Block Method

The guidelines below will help you remember what you need to do in each part of a comparison/contrast essay using the block method.

Introduction

1. Provide background information about your topic.
2. Identify the two things being compared and contrasted.
3. State the purpose for making the comparison and/or contrast.
4. Write a thesis statement that states the focus of your essay.

Supporting Paragraphs

1. In the first paragraph(s), discuss the similarities.
2. In the next paragraph(s), discuss the differences.

Conclusion

1. Restate the purpose for comparison and/or contrast in different words.
2. Summarize the main similarities and differences.
3. Draw a conclusion.

Point-by-Point Method

The guidelines below will help you remember what you need to do in each section of a comparison/contrast essay using the point-by-point method.

Introduction

1. Provide background information about your topic.
2. Identify the two things being compared and contrasted.
3. State the purpose for making the comparison and/or contrast.
4. Identify the points to be compared and contrasted.
5. Write a thesis statement that states the focus of your essay.

Supporting Paragraphs

1. In the first paragraph, compare and/or contrast the two things according to the first point you identified.
2. In the second paragraph, compare and/or contrast the two things according to the second point you identified.
3. Do the same thing in the third and subsequent paragraphs.

Conclusion

1. Restate the purpose for comparison and/or contrast in different words.
2. Summarize the main similarities and differences.
3. Draw a conclusion.

> **tip** When you use the point-by-point method to write about similarities or differences, you need to decide how you are going to order the points. Again, one common way is to organize the points according to order of importance. For example, you can begin with the most important point and end with the least important point.

Writing an Essay of Comparison and Contrast: Block Method

In this activity, you will practice writing an essay of comparison and contrast. Follow these steps:

Prewriting

A. Choose one of the following topics and use the space below to brainstorm a list of similarities and differences.

- Compare and contrast yourself and another member of your family.
- Compare and contrast some aspect of your culture, such as eating habits, education, government, economy, religion, or social life, with the same aspect of another culture.
- Compare and contrast a photo and a painting of the same scene.
- Compare and contrast two people you have worked with, such as two co-workers at a job, two students in a group, two secretaries you have known, or two bosses you have had.
- Your own topic

B. Organize your list by grouping the similarities in one group and the differences in another group. Then prepare an informal outline for your essay. Be sure that you have identified a purpose for making your comparison. For example, are you comparing two restaurants so that you can recommend one of them to a friend? Are you comparing your native language and English to show why English is easy or difficult for you to learn? Develop your essay according to your purpose.

Writing

On a separate piece of paper, write the first draft of your essay. Use the essay plan on page 59 to help you write your draft. Be sure to provide some background information in the introduction and include a clear thesis statement that states your purpose for comparison. Organize the supporting paragraphs so that all the similarities are in one paragraph and all the differences are in another paragraph. End with a conclusion that restates your purpose for the comparison and that summarizes the main similarities and differences.

Revising and Editing

A. *Personal Revising. Wait at least one day, and then revise your essay. Also, check to make sure you have provided enough support to explain fully the similarities and differences. Write or type a revised version of your essay.*

B. *Peer Revising. Exchange drafts with a partner. Use the following worksheet as a guide for suggesting improvements in your partner's essay.*

Writer: ____________________ Peer Editor: ____________________

1. Did the introduction identify the two items being compared? ____ yes ____ no
2. Is the purpose of the comparison clearly stated? ____ yes ____ no
3. Did the introduction make you want to read the rest of the essay? ____ yes ____ no

   Why or why not? ____

   ____

   ____

4. Did the author adequately develop the points of comparison in a paragraph? ____ yes ____ no

   If not, how can the paragraph be strengthened? ____________________

   ____

   ____

5. Did the author adequately develop the points of contrast in another paragraph? ____ yes ____ no

   If not, how can the paragraph be strengthened? ____________________

   ____

6. Did the author include an effective conclusion? ____ yes ____ no

   If not, how can it be improved? ____________________

   ____

   ____

Incorporate any suggestions your partner has made that you agree with.

C. *Editing. Correct all the grammar, punctuation, capitalization, and spelling errors before you copy it over or type it.*

Explore the Web

Think of something you would like to buy such as a new television, car, sewing machine, camera, etc. Explore the Web to find two examples of that product that you could purchase on the Internet. Read the descriptions of the two items and make a list of the similarities and differences between them. For example, you can compare and contrast the price, size, quality, and features of the two items.

You Be the Editor

The following paragraph contains nine mistakes. Find the mistakes and correct them.

Now that I am pregnant with our first child, my husband and I will have to find a bigger place to live. Our little apartment in the city is too small for three people. We trying to decide whether we should get a biggest apartment in the city or move to the suburbs. We have four main considerations expense, space, convenience, and schools. In general, is probably expensiver to live in the city. On the other hand, we would have to buy a car if we moved to the suburbs we would also have to buy a lawnmower and a snowblower or hire someone care for the lawn and driveway. In terms of space, we could definitely have a bigger house and much more land if we lived in the suburbs. However, we wonder if it would be worth it, since we would lose so many conveniences. Stores would be farther away, and so would friends, neighbors, movie theaters, museums, and restaurants. The most biggest inconvenience would be that we would both have to commute to work every day instead of walking or taking the bus. The Schools are probably better in the suburbs, but for our child, who isn't even born yet, school is several years away. In looking at our priorities, it becomes clear that we should continue to live in the city for now and then reevaluate our decision as the baby gets closer to school age.

On Your Own

Write a comparison/contrast essay using the point-by-point method. Choose one of the topics below and identify several points on which to base your comparison. Follow the five steps of good writing as you write your essay, and be sure that you have a clear purpose for your comparison.

1. Compare and contrast two items such as a computer and a typewriter, glasses and contact lenses, a CD and a cassette tape, or a VCR and a DVD.
2. Compare and contrast dating customs in your generation and your grandparents' generation.
3. Your own topic

Unit Three Above material from: *Ready to Write More*

Timed Reading

Time yourself to see how long it takes you to read the following selection. To increase your reading rate and comprehension, try not to read one word at a time. Try to read the words in groups or phrases.

Compare your results to the timed reading you did in the first Unit of this book. How much did you improve? What are some things you can continue to do to help increase your reading rate and improve your comprehension?

Do You Speak British or American?

Starting time ________

American and British people both speak English, of course, but sometimes it doesn't seem like the same language. In fact, there are some important differences between British and American English.

First of all, they sound very different. Often, Americans don't say all the letters in each word, especially consonants like "t" and "d." For example, Americans may say "I dunno" instead of "I don't know," or they may say "Whaddya say?" instead of "What do you say?" However, the British usually pronounce their consonants more carefully.

Also, some letters have different sounds. For example, Americans say the "a" in "half" like the "a" in "cat," but the British say the "a" in "half like the "a" in "aah." The "r" is sometimes said differently, too. Most Americans say both the "r"s in "farmer," but most British people don't. The British say "fahmah."

Sound is not the only difference between British English and American English. The two languages have different words for some things. For example, the words for clothing are different. Americans use the word "sweater," but the British say "jumper." Americans wear "vests" over their shirts, but in England they wear "vests" under their shirts. Americans wear "pants" over their "underpants," but the British wear "pants" under their "trousers."

Many other words and expressions are different in the two countries. In England, if you are going to telephone a friend, you "ring her up." In America, you "give her a call." The British use the word "lovely" to describe something they like. Americans use the word "cool" or "great." If an American says someone is "mad" they mean "angry." If a Englishman says someone is "mad" they mean "crazy."

There are also some differences in grammar. For example, Americans almost always use the helping verb "do" with the verb "have." They might say "Do you have an extra pen?" The British often ask the question a different way. They might say "Have you got an extra pen?"

These differences can be confusing if you are learning English. But there is a reason for the differences. Languages change over time. When the same language is used in different places, it changes differently in each place. This is what happened to English. It also happened to other languages, such as French. Many people in Canada speak French, but their French is different from the French spoken in France.

(400 words)

Finishing time ______________ **Reading time** ______________

Answer the questions on the following page.

READING RATE TABLE

Reading Time (Minutes: Seconds)	Rate (Words per Minute)	Reading Time (Minutes: Seconds)	Rate (Words per Minute)
:30 sec	800 wpm		
:35	686	2:10	185
:40	597	2:15	178
:45	533	2:20	172
:50	480	2:25	166
:55	440	2:30	160
1:00	400	2:35	155
1:05	370	2:40	149
1:10	345	2:45	145
1:15	320	2:50	141
1:20	300	2:55	137
1:25	282	3:00	133
1:30	267	3:15	123
1:35	253	3:30	114
1:40	240	3:45	107
1:45	229	4:00	100
1:50	219	4:15	94
1:55	209	4:30	89
2:00	200	4:45	84
2:05	192	5:00	80

Reading/Writing—Fielding

Circle the best answer. Do not look back!

1. This passage is about
   a. some of the words American people use.
   b. the way British people say certain words.
   c. how American sounds are different from British sounds.
   d. how American English is different from British English.
2. When Americans speak, you often don't hear
   a. any consonant sounds.
   b. some consonant sounds.
   c. any vowel sounds.
   d. any words at all.
3. In the United States and England, some letters
   a. always sound the same.
   b. have different sounds.
   c. sound like French.
   d. have an unusual sound.
4. The words for clothing are
   a. an example of British English.
   b. an example of modern technology.
   c. different in the United States and England.
   d. very difficult to learn in English.
5. People in the United States and in England
   a. always use the same expressions.
   b. often say good-bye to each other.
   c. don't use expressions often.
   d. sometimes use different expressions.
6. When Americans ask questions, they usually
   a. use the helping verb *do*.
   b. don't use a helping verb.
   c. don't use any grammar.
   d. cause some confusion.
7. English learners can get confused because
   a. English never changes.
   b. it is different in different places.
   c. people often ask them questions.
   d. the French language is different.
8. Languages
   a. change over time.
   b. are difficult.
   c. don't change much.
   d. are the same in all places.

Unit Four

Stress and Anxiety

Learning to Learn

In this chapter you will read about some different aspects of education. Reading A is about test anxiety, which most students experience at some time in their educational career. Reading B describes a boy's fear of the unknown.

In this chapter, you will practice:

READING SKILLS

- Previewing a reading
- Understanding main ideas
- Reading between the lines

VOCABULARY SKILLS

- Using context clues to understand vocabulary
- Previewing vocabulary
- Choosing the correct word form

LIFE SKILLS

- Setting realistic goals

Section I: Reading

Reading A: How to Reduce Test Anxiety

Before You Read

Previewing

Work in small groups. Discuss the questions.

1. How do you prepare for a big test? Do you stay up late at night trying to study?
2. How do you feel the morning before a test?
3. How do you feel as you turn over the question sheet and begin to answer the questions?
4. How do you feel after the test?

Using Context Clues to Understand Vocabulary

The words in bold print are in Reading A. Guess the meaning of each word by looking at the context. Circle the letter of the best answer.

1. When the body is very hot, it produces a liquid that forms on the skin. **Sweating** cools the skin and therefore cools the person. If you are perspiring a lot, it is important to drink a lot of water to replace the liquid the body is losing.
   a. exercising
   b. drinking water
   c. perspiring
2. Some people suffer from an **abnormal** fear of spiders. They cannot even look at a spider without feeling very frightened.
   a. common
   b. unusual
   c. stupid
3. Last night I was really embarrassed. I met an old friend at a party, but when I introduced her to my husband, I suddenly **went blank**. I just couldn't remember her name.
   a. was unable to remember anything
   b. felt dizzy
   c. felt very embarrassed

4. **Focusing** on your illness is not a good thing. Instead, you should try to think about getting better and how you will feel then.
   a. getting medical treatment
   b. thinking hard about something
   c. talking about
5. If you find someone who is unconscious, it is **vital** that you call 911 and, if necessary, begin CPR. If you don't do this, the person may die.
   a. a little bit important
   b. extremely important
   c. a good idea
6. "You look really tired!"

   "I am. I forgot about the math test today, so I spent all last night **cramming** for it. Now I'm so tired, I can't remember anything I learned."
   a. studying in a sensible way
   b. worrying about something such as a test
   c. learning a lot of information fast
7. The English teacher asked the class to write a story about their lives. He told them to organize their writing **chronologically**, beginning with their first memory as a child and ending at the present time.
   a. neatly and correctly
   b. organized into paragraphs
   c. arranged according to when something happened
8. When I asked my son to think about some **realistic goals**, he told me he had a goal: He was going to work hard to try to win the lottery. I explained that this was not a realistic goal. Instead, I asked him to think about improving his grades at school and keeping his room tidy.
   a. something you want to do and can do in the future
   b. something that is impossible to do in the future
   c. something that will help your parents in the future

Reading A:

How to Reduce Test Anxiety

1 Most teachers agree that it is normal to feel some nervousness or tension before a test. In fact, you usually perform better when you are a little nervous, because you try harder. So feeling nervous is a healthy and natural part of test taking. However, it is not healthy to feel so nervous that you go blank when you read the questions. It is also not normal to feel physically ill—to worry so much that you feel sick or dizzy. If you are this nervous, you are suffering from test anxiety.

2 How do you know whether you are suffering from normal nervousness or test anxiety? People experience different symptoms. Specific physical symptoms of test anxiety include:

- sweating
- having headaches
- feeling sick
- feeling dizzy
- having an abnormal heartbeat

Mental or emotional symptoms of test anxiety include:

- going blank
- feeling stupid and worthless
- reading without understanding
- worrying that everyone else is better than you
- focusing on failing, not on passing

3 We can divide test anxiety into two kinds: normal and abnormal. If you have not prepared for the test properly, and you don't know or don't understand the material, it is completely normal to feel test anxiety. In other words, if you haven't studied well and don't know any of the answers, it is normal to feel physically ill. If, however, you have studied well throughout the class and you have prepared carefully for the test, but you still suffer symptoms of test anxiety, then this is not normal. You need to learn to overcome these feelings so that you can show the teacher exactly how much you have learned. In both situations, there are some simple steps that will help you overcome this anxiety and do better in tests.

4 Preparation is vital in test taking. It does not start the night before a test, however. Cramming at the last minute and staying up all night before the test is never the best way to study. You should prepare by taking good notes throughout the class and keeping those notes neatly in a chronologically organized binder. You must also keep up with your work and, very importantly, make an appointment to see the teacher if you don't understand something. Good students meet with their teachers for help once or twice throughout the course. The teachers usually have helpful suggestions about improving understanding. As the test date gets nearer, make a plan of what you need to review, or look over again. Try to predict what will be on the test and add this to your plan. Show your plan to your teacher to see if you are on the right track.

5 Another important part of preparation is setting realistic goals. In most schools, grades are very important. It is normal to worry about your grade and to want a high grade. However, some students want to get 100% on every test and in every subject, and they feel depressed if they get a lower score. They put an enormous amount of pressure on themselves to be perfect, and most of us cannot be perfect all the time in every subject. So be realistic. Try to do the best you can, but don't always try to be perfect.

6 All students learn better and will suffer less anxiety if they set realistic goals and learn as they go. Research also shows that learners remember and understand information better and for longer periods of time if they write the information down instead of just trying to remember it. Preparing for a test is a skill, and you can easily learn how to do it well. Then, when that test comes along, you will be able to show the teacher how much you have learned rather than how nervous you are.

After You Read

How Well Did You Read?

Read the statements. Write T *(true),* F*(false), or* N *(not enough information).*

_____ 1. It is normal to feel nervous before a test.

_____ 2. Everyone suffering from test anxiety feels dizzy and goes blank.

_____ 3. You can learn how to reduce test anxiety.

_____ 4. Trying to get 100% on every test is an unrealistic goal.

Discussing the Reading

Work in small groups. Talk about the questions.

1. Paragraph 1 says that it is helpful to feel a little nervous in a test. Do you agree?
2. Do you experience any of the physical or mental symptoms mentioned in paragraph 2? What do you do during a test if you feel sick or go blank?
3. This reading says that cramming all night before a test is not a good idea. Do you agree? Have you ever crammed the night before a test? If so, did you pass the test?
4. This reading is in the last chapter of this book. You will probably have an end-of-course test soon. How are you preparing for that test? Do you know what kind of test you will have? Have you begun to study? Are you planning to cram the night before?

Check Your Understanding

Circle the letter of the best answer.

1. What is the main idea of the first paragraph?
   a. Although it is normal to feel a little nervous before a test, it is not normal to experience test anxiety if you have prepared well.
   b. Feeling nervous is a healthy and natural part of test taking.
   c. If you are very nervous, you are suffering from depression.
2. Which symptom of test anxiety is this student suffering from?
   "When I am taking a test, I look around and see that all my friends are writing very quickly. I'm just not as good as they are."
   a. going blank
   b. feeling dizzy
   c. worrying that everyone else is better than you

3. Which symptom of test anxiety is this person suffering from?

   "If I don't pass this class, my parents will be so mad. Maybe I can tell them I am really sick."

   a. feeling stupid and worthless
   b. focusing on failing, not on passing
   c. feeling sick

4. Which is an example of abnormal test anxiety according to this reading?

   a. "My mind went blank, even though I stayed up all night studying for this test."
   b. "I started sweating and feeling dizzy. All the weeks of preparation disappeared, and my mind went blank."
   c. "My heart started beating fast, and I felt very sick when I saw that the test was about a book I'd forgotten to read."

5. How is paragraph 4 organized?

   a. It compares different ways of preparing for a test.
   b. It describes a series of steps in a process.
   c. It contrasts different ways of preparing for a test.

6. Some students feel depressed if they get 85% in a test because __________

   a. this is a very low grade.
   b. this is a good grade.
   c. they have unrealistic goals.

7. What would be an example of a realistic goal for most people?

   a. "I want to travel around the world by the time I am thirty."
   b. "I want to have a part-time job that will give me good experience while I'm at college."
   c. "I want to get A's in every subject this year at college."

8. What is the opposite of cramming according to the last paragraph?

   a. learning as you go
   b. setting realistic goals
   c. understanding how you learn

Choosing the Correct Word Form

A. Work with a partner. Read the words aloud. Reading A uses one or more forms of these words. Quickly scan the reading to find and underline the words. Talk about their meaning.

Verbs	Nouns	Adjectives
1.	anxiety	anxious
2. feel	feeling	
3. prepare	preparation	
4. study	student	studious
5. organize	organization	organized
6. suggest	suggestion	
7. inform	information	informative
8. perform	performance	

B. Choose the best word form to complete each sentence. When you use a verb, use the correct tense and make the verb agree with its subject. The number in the table above corresponds to the question number.

1. The student felt very ***anxious*** before the test. Her ***anxiety*** was so bad she felt dizzy and sick.
2. "Don't you have any ______________ for me?" the actor cried. "Yes," replied the actress quietly. "I ______________ sorry for you."
3. I didn't know about the test, so I didn't ______________ for it. My lack of ______________ earned me a failing grade.
4. My friend is very ______________. Every night he ______________ for two hours before dinner.
5. Juan's binder wasn't ______________ at all. His papers were all over the place and he couldn't find anything. He decided to ______________ his binder during lunch break.

6. "What can we do today?" asked Peter.

   "Let's go to the movies," his friend ______________________

   "I have a better ______________________. Let's stay home and rent a movie."
7. There is a lot of good ______________________ about learning English on the Web. Our college, for example, has a very ______________________ Web site.
8. Most people ______________________ better on a test if they have had a good night's sleep. If they are tired, their ______________________ can suffer.

C. Complete the sentences using your own words.

1. It was after midnight and I was anxious because ______________________.
2. "How do you feel today?" asked the doctor.

   "I have a ______________________."
3. Preparation is very important if ______________________.
4. I didn't prepare for the test, so last night I studied ______________________.
5. I must organize my ______________________.
6. The student had a good suggestion: "Let's ______________________."
7. I am so excited! My teacher has just informed me ______________________.
8. Sam's performance in class was not very good. He often ______________________

   ______________________.

Reading B: A Day's Wait

Follow these steps:

1. The title of this story is "A Day's Wait." The author is Ernest Hemingway. Before you read, talk with another student. What do you think the story is about? How can you tell? Write your guess here.

   ____

2. Read the story all the way to the end. Don't stop for new words. (You'll have another chance to read the story.)
3. Talk about the story with another student. Ask each other:
   - Where does the story take place?
   - Who are the people in the story?
   - What happens in the story?
   - Was any part of the story hard to understand?
4. Read the story again. Mark with a pencil the new words that you want to learn.
5. Talk to another student about the new words. Guess the meanings. Write them here.

   ____

   ____

   ____

   ____

   ____

   ____

   ____

6. Work with a group of three or four students. Retell the story from beginning to end. Then ask each other these questions:
   - Did you like the story? Why?
   - Did you like the ending? Why?
   - Can you think of a different ending?
   - Have you ever had trouble with different ways of measuring things?

A Day's Wait

by Ernest Hemingway

He came into the room to shut the windows while we were still in bed and I saw he looked ill. He was shivering, his face was white, and he walked slowly as though it ached to move.

"What's the matter, Schatz?"

"I've got a headache."

"You better go back to bed."

"No. I'm all right."

"You go to bed. I'll see you when I'm dressed."

But when I came downstairs he was dressed, sitting by the fire, looking a very sick and miserable boy of nine years. When I put my hand on his forehead I knew he had a fever.

"You go up to bed," I said, "you're sick."

"I'm all right," he said.

When the doctor came he took the boy's temperature.

"What is it?" I asked him.

"One hundred and two."

Downstairs, the doctor left three different medicines in different colored capsules with instructions for giving them. One was to bring down the fever, another a purgative, the third to overcome an acid condition. The germs of influenza can only exist in an acid condition, he explained. He seemed to know all about influenza and said there was nothing to worry about if the fever did not go above one hundred and four degrees. This was a light epidemic of flu and there was no danger if you avoided pneumonia.

Back in the room I wrote the boy's temperature down and made a note of the time to give the various capsules.

"Do you want me to read to you?"

"All right. If you want to," said the boy. His face was very white and there were dark areas under his eyes. He lay still in the bed and seemed very detached from what was going on.

I read aloud from Howard Pyle's *Book of Pirates;* but I could see he was not following what I was reading.

"How do you feel, Schatz?" I asked him.

"Just the same, so far," he said.

I sat at the foot of the bed and read to myself while I waited for it to be time to give another capsule. It would have been natural for him to go to sleep, but when I looked up he was looking at the foot of the bed, looking very strangely.

"Why don't you try to go to sleep? I'll wake you up for the medicine."

"I'd rather stay awake."

After a while he said to me, "You don't have to stay in here with me, Papa, if it bothers you."

"It doesn't bother me."

"No, I mean you don't have to stay if it's going to bother you."

I thought perhaps he was a little lightheaded and after giving him the prescribed capsules at eleven o'clock I went out for a while.

It was a bright, cold day, the ground covered with a sleet that had frozen so that it seemed as if all the bare trees, the bushes, the cut brush and all the grass and the bare ground had been varnished with ice. I took the young Irish setter for a little walk up the road and along a frozen creek, but it was difficult to stand or walk on the glassy surface and the red dog slipped and slithered and I fell twice, hard, once dropping my gun and having it slide away over the ice.

We flushed a covey of quail under a high clay bank with overhanging brush and I killed two as they went out of sight over the top of the bank. Some of the covey lit in trees, but most of them scattered into brush piles and it was necessary to jump on the ice-coated mounds of brush several times before they would flush. Coming out while you were poised unsteadily on the icy, springy brush they made difficult shooting and I killed two, missed five, and started back pleased to have found a covey close to the house and happy there were so many left to find another day.

At the house they said the boy had refused to let anyone come into the room.

"You can't come in," he said. "You mustn't get what I have."

I went up to him and found him in exactly the position I had left him, white-faced, but with the tops of his cheeks flushed by the fever, staring still, as he stared, at the foot of the bed.

I took his temperature.

"What is it?"

"Something like a hundred," I said. It was one hundred and two and four tenths.

"It was a hundred and two," he said.

"Who said so?"

"The doctor."

"Your temperature is all right," I said. "It's nothing to worry about."

"I don't worry," he said, "but I can't keep from thinking."

"Don't think," I said. "Just take it easy."

"I'm taking it easy," he said and looked straight ahead. He was evidently holding tight onto himself about something.

"Take this with water."

"Do you think it will do any good?"

"Of course it will."

I sat down and opened the Pirate book and commenced to read, but I could see he was not following, so I stopped.

"About what time do you think I'm going to die?" he asked.

"What?"

"About how long will it be before I die?"

"You aren't going to die. What's the matter with you?"

"Oh, yes, I am. I heard him say a hundred and two."

"People don't die with a fever of one hundred and two. That's a silly way to talk."

"I know they do. At school in France the boys told me you can't live with forty-four degrees. I've got a hundred and two."

He had been waiting to die all day, ever since nine o'clock in the morning.

"You poor Schatz," I said. "Poor old Schatz. It's like miles and kilometers. You aren't going to die. That's a different thermometer. On that thermometer thirty-seven is normal. On this kind it's ninety-eight."

"Are you sure?"

"Absolutely," I said. "It's like miles and kilometers. You know, like how many kilometers we make when we do seventy miles in the car?"

"Oh," he said.

But his gaze at the foot of the bed relaxed slowly. The hold over himself relaxed too, finally, and the next day it was very slack and he cried very easily at little things that were of no importance.

Appendix A

Choosing a Pleasure Reading Book

Finding Good Books

Now you will choose a book of your own to read. You can find a good book from the book list on pages 79–82. The books on this list are not difficult to read, and they are popular with English speakers. You can find them in many libraries and bookstores.

The books on the list are just suggestions. You don't have to read one of these books. However, if you want to read a book that is not on the list, check with your teacher. If the book is too easy or too difficult, you won't enjoy it. You can find many other good and not-too-difficult books in the Young Adult section of bookstores or libraries.

You can also find books written for English learners. These are called *graded readers*. They are often easier to read, especially if you are not used to reading in English. However, they may also be less interesting than books for English speakers. You should look at them carefully before choosing one. You may find some of these books in your classroom or in the school library. If you want to read a graded reader, start with level 2 or 3.

Previewing a Book

When you find a book that interests you, preview it. This means you should look at it carefully, following these steps:

1. Read the front cover and back cover of the book. Does it seem interesting?
2. How long is it? A short book is better to start with.
3. Are there any pictures? In a nonfiction book, pictures can help you understand.
4. Check to make sure that the book is not too difficult or too easy. Read one page. If you know all the words on the page, the book may be too easy. If you find more than ten new words, the book may be too difficult for you.
5. Remember: ***The book should be interesting to you.*** It should not be something you think you *should* read. It should be something you *want* to read!

Getting the Most from Pleasure Reading

- Read your book every day. On a separate page in your notebook, keep a record of the number of pages you read each day. Try to read your book quickly.

- You may find some new words in your book. Don't use a dictionary for every new word. Try to guess the meaning or skip over the word. If you use a dictionary often, you won't be able to follow the story.
- After you finish the book, tell your teacher. She may talk to you about it. She may ask you to tell the class or write about your book.
- If you liked your book, tell a friend about it, too.
- Keep a record of the books you read.

Book List

This list has two main sections: **Fiction** and **Nonfiction**. Fiction books are not true stories. The stories are made up by the authors. Nonfiction books are written to give facts and information. They are about every kind of topic: biography, history, travel, adventure, nature, science, and many others.

Fiction

A Lantern in Her Hand, by Bess Streeter Aldrich. The story of Abby MacKenzie Deal, who lived in the American West during the Civil War. (251 pages)

Under the Domim Tree, by Gila Almagor. Three teenage girls learn to become women in 1953 in Israel. (164 pages)

Sometimes I Think I Hear My Name, by Avi. The story of a thirteen-year-old boy who tries to understand his parents. Humorous. (139 pages)

If Beale Street Could Talk, by James Baldwin. The story of a young black American family. A man is in jail, but he did not do anything wrong. A sad love story. (197 pages)

The Squared Circle, by James Bennett. Sonny Youngblood is a star basketball player. But who is he, really? (247 pages)

Forever, by Judy Blume. The famous story of teenage love. The question is, can you love two people at the same time? A best-seller. (220 pages)

Paper Moon, by Joe David Brown. The story of an eleven-year-old girl in the American South during the 1930 Depression years. (308 pages)

SOS Titanic, by Eve Bunting. A young man tries to rescue his friends as the ship *Titanic* sinks into the cold sea. (246 pages)

The Incredible Journey, by Sheila Burnford. Two dogs and a cat travel many miles to return to their home. (146 pages)

The White Mountains, by John Christopher. One hundred years from now, Switzerland is the only free country. This is science fiction and a thriller. (214 pages)

The House on Mango Street, by Sandra Cisneros. Esperánza is a young girl growing up in the Hispanic section of Chicago. She learns to make a happy life in the middle of broken-down buildings and personal difficulties. (110 pages)

Me, Too, by Vera and Bill Cleaver. A twelve-year-old girl tries to help her twin sister. (158 pages)

Where the Lilies Bloom, by Vera and Bill Cleaver. A young girl keeps her brothers and sisters together after both of their parents die. Set in the Great Smoky Mountains in the American South. (175 pages)

The Chocolate War, by Robert Cormier. A student fights a secret society of other students and becomes a hero in the school. (191 pages)

Children of the River, by Linda Crew. Sundara has fled Cambodia and is now living in Oregon, trying to be a "good Cambodian girl" in America. (213 pages)

I Know What You Did Last Summer, by Lois Duncan. A horror story about a secret. (198 pages)

Ransom, by Lois Duncan. Five students take a strange and scary bus ride. (172 pages)

The Slave Dancer, by Paula Fox. A boy finds himself on a slave ship, a place of horrible violence and cruelty. (152 pages)

The Autobiography of Miss Jane Pittman, by Ernest J. Gaines. The story of an American black woman born during the days of slavery. Later in her life, she saw black people get freedom. (245 pages)

Julie of the Wolves, by Jean Craighead George. Julie, an Eskimo girl, is to be married at the age of thirteen. She runs away, makes friends with a wolf pack, and survives. (170 pages)

The Miracle Worker, by William Gibson. A play about Annie Sullivan and how she helped a blind girl named Helen Keller. (122 pages)

Morning Is a Long Time Coming, by Bette Greene. A young American finds adventure and love in Paris after World War II. (261 pages)

Summer of My German Soldier, by Bette Greene. A friendship between a young Jewish girl and a German prisoner in America. (199 pages)

The Drowning of Stephan Jones, by Bette Greene. Stephan and his friends hate gay couples, especially two men who live nearby. His girlfriend, Carla, doesn't know what to think. Then Stephan drowns himself. (217 pages)

The Friends, by Rosa Guy. A family moves to the United States from the West Indies. This story tells about the love and friendship they find. (185 pages)

Ruby, by Rosa Guy. The problems of an eighteen-year-old girl as she tries to become a woman. (186 pages)

Zed, by Rosemary Harris. A young boy tells the story of his experience as a hostage of political terrorists. (185 pages)

The Old Man and the Sea, by Ernest Hemingway. A lonely, old fisherman struggles to catch a big fish. Then he has to fight off the sharks who want to eat it. A young boy is with him. (140 pages)

Jazz Country, by Nat Hentoff. Life in New York City is tough for a young musician. (146 pages)

This School Is Driving Me Crazy, by Nat Hentoff. More about life in New York City. (154 pages)

Letters from Rifka, by Karen Hesse. Rifka and her family have to leave Russia in 1919, and then her family has to leave her. (147 pages)

Rumblefish, by S. E. Hinton. Rusty wants to be tough, like his older brother, but he gets into trouble. (122 pages)

That Was Then, This Is Now, by S. E. Hinton. Sixteen-year-olds Mark and Bryon were like brothers. But now they begin to grow apart. (159 pages)

Gentlehands, by M. E. Kerr. A policeman's son falls in love with a rich girl and then they discover an ex-Nazi in the family. (135 pages)

Night Shift, by Stephen King. Twenty horror stories to make you afraid of the dark. A best-seller! (326 pages)

I Want to Keep My Baby, by Joanna Lee. A fifteen-year-old girl is going to have a baby. (166 pages)

Very Far Away from Anywhere Else, by Ursula K. LeGuin. A young man wants to become a scientist, but his parents want him to be like everyone else. (87 pages)

The Lion, the Witch, and the Wardrobe, by C. S. Lewis. Three children climb into a wardrobe and find a strange new world when they go through the back of it. For readers who like fantasy. (154 pages)

The Contender, by Robert Lipsyte. Alfred, a high-school dropout, wants to be a champion boxer. Then he learns a very important lesson. (167 pages)

A Summer to Die, by Lois Lowry. The story of a young girl whose sister dies of leukemia. (120 pages)

Anne of Green Gables, by Lucy Maud Montgomery. The beloved classic story of a red-haired, lively orphan girl who is loved by everyone she meets. (310 pages)

The Dog Who Wouldn't Be, by Farley Mowat. A funny story about an unusual dog. (195 pages)

The Boat Who Wouldn't Float, by Farley Mowat. Another funny story by a very amusing writer. (241 pages)

No Turning Back, by Beverly Naidoo. A boy in South Africa runs away to the city and lives on the streets. (189 pages)

Edgar Allen, by John Neufeld. A white American family adopts a black child. (128 pages)

Lisa, Bright and Dark, by John Neufeld. A sixteen-year-old girl knows she is losing control of her thoughts and feelings. But no one believes her except her three good friends, who help her. (143 pages)

The Black Pearl, by Scott O'Dell. Ramon wants to find the "Pearl of Heaven" in order to show how good a diver he is. Ramon finds the pearl, but he learns an important lesson. (140 pages)

Animal Farm, by George Orwell. The animals are not happy on the farm. They send away the humans and run the farm themselves. Is their life any better? Read and find out! (132 pages)

The Light in the Forest, by Conrad Richter. A white boy is raised by American Indians in Pennsylvania. This book tells about early life in the United States. (117 pages)

Harry Potter and the Sorcerer's Stone (Harry Potter and the Philosopher's Stone), by J. K. Rowling. The adventures of a boy who discovers that he is a wizard. Very entertaining and exciting. (312 pages)

Shane, by Jack Schaefer. A stranger helps a family in the American West. He teaches a young boy courage and self-respect. (119 pages)

My Name Is Davy—I'm an Alcoholic, by Anne Snyder. A lonely high-school student drinks too much. (128 pages)

The Pearl, by John Steinbeck. A poor fisherman finds a big pearl and hopes to get rich by selling it. Can a pearl bring happiness to his family? (118 pages)

Sons from Afar, by Cynthia Voigt. Two brothers are very different from each other, but both wish they could find their father. (263 pages)

Wrestling Sturbridge, by Rick Wallace. A young wrestler in a small town wants to be the champion. (134 pages)

A Boat to Nowhere, by Maureen Crane Wartski. Kien is a young Vietnamese boy who is trying to escape from the government. This is his story. (191 pages)

My Brother, My Sister, and I, by Yoko Kawashima Watkins. A family struggles in poverty in war-torn Japan. Then the brother is accused of murder! (233 pages)

Charlotte's Web, by E. B. White. Written for children, this book is popular with all ages. It tells a story of love and loyalty that everyone can understand. (184 pages)

Nonfiction

Go Ask Alice, by Anonymous. The true story of a fifteen-year-old girl who became addicted to drugs. She tells how and why it happened. (188 pages)

New Burlington: The Life and Death of an American Village, by John Baskin. A village is moved to make way for a new lake. The people from the village tell their own stories. (259 pages)

Sacajawea, by Joseph Bruchai. This is the story of a young American Indian woman. She helped the explorers Lewis and Clark find a way to the Pacific Ocean. (199 pages)

There Comes a Time: The Struggle for Civil Rights, by Milton Meltzer. This is an easy-to-read book about the civil rights movement in the 1960s in the United States. (180 pages)

J. R. R. Tolkien: The Man Who Created the Lord of the Rings, by Michael Coren. Tolkien's life was not easy. He was an orphan and a soldier. Later, he was a professor. He used his life experiences to write his books. (125 pages)

Boy, by Roald Dahl. This famous writer tells about his childhood and his unhappy experiences in school in England. (176 pages)

The Double Life of Pocahontas, by Jean Fritz. Pocahontas was an American Indian girl who grew up in a white family. Then she went back to live with her own people. (85 pages)

Homesick, by Jean Fritz. The true story of her early life in China and how her family had to leave suddenly because of the war. (163 pages)

Red Scarf Girl, by Ji-Li Jiang. Ji-Li remembers when she was a girl during the Cultural Revolution in China. (285 pages)

Rosa Parks: My Story, by Rosa Parks with Jim Haskins. On December 1, 1953, Mrs. Parks was on a bus in the U.S. South. She refused to give up her seat to a white man. As a result, the U.S. civil rights movement began. (188 pages)

The Upstairs Room, by Johanna Reiss. How two Jewish sisters lived with a Christian family during World War II in Holland. (196 pages)

J. K. Rowling: The Wizard Behind Harry Potter, by Marc Shapiro. This is the life story of one of the most successful writers of our time. (163 pages)

Almost Lost, by Beatrice Sparks. The true story of an anonymous teenager's life on the streets of a big city. (239 pages)

It Happened to Nancy, by Beatrice Sparks. A true story from Nancy's diary. She thought she had found love, but instead she found AIDS. (238 pages)

Helen Keller: From Tragedy to Triumph, by Katherine E. Wilkie. Helen became deaf and blind when she was a small child. This is the story of her success as a student, a writer, and a lecturer. (192 pages)

Appendix B
Organization

Overview of Essay Organization

A paragraph is a group of sentences about one topic and has three main parts: the topic sentence, the body (supporting sentences), and the concluding sentence. Similarly, an essay is a group of paragraphs about one topic and also has three main parts: the introduction, the body, and the conclusion. The diagram below shows that a paragraph and an essay have the same basic plan; an essay is just longer.

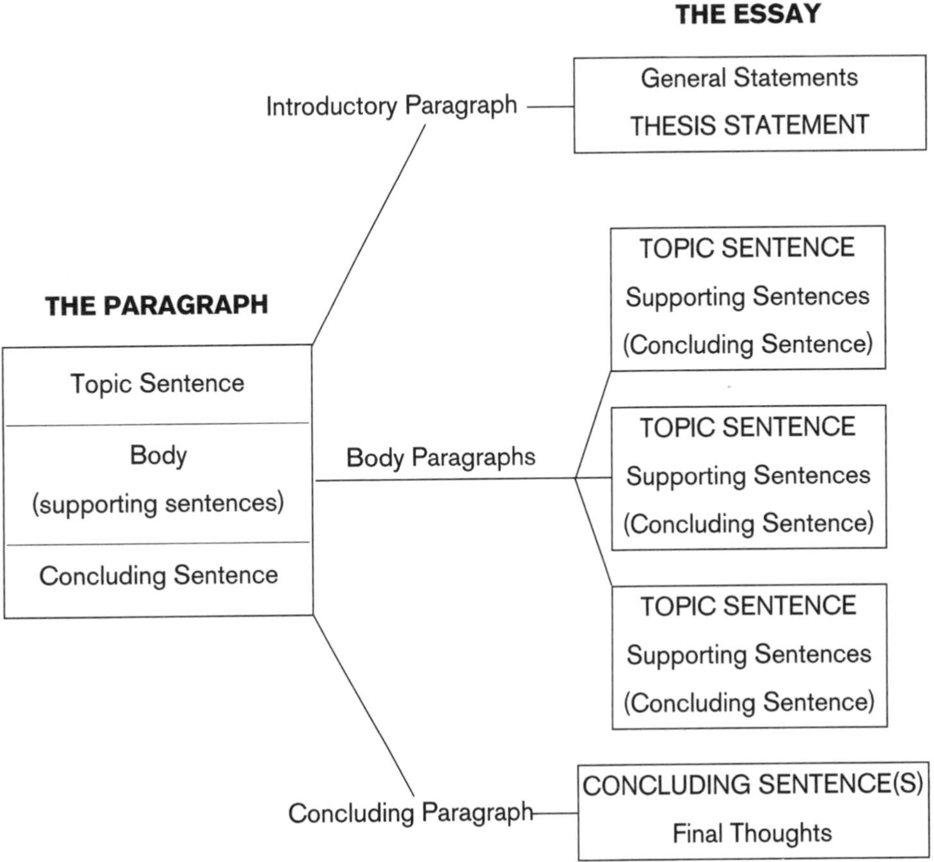

Let's examine each part of the essay.

The Introductory Paragraph

The introduction is the first paragraph of the essay. It introduces the topic of the essay and arouses the reader's interest. There are several ways to write an introductory paragraph. In this book, you will learn to write a "funnel introduction." A funnel introduction has two parts: several general statements and one thesis statement.

General statements give the reader background information about the topic of the essay. They should lead your reader gradually from a very general idea of your topic to a very specific idea. The first general statement in a funnel introduction just introduces the topic. Like the lens of a camera moving in for a close-up picture, each sentence that follows becomes more and more focused on a specific topic. There is no exact rule about the number of general statements you need; however, you should try to write at least three or four, and they should be interesting enough to hold the reader's attention. It is permissible to sprinkle a few interesting details in the general statements in order to attract the reader's interest. However, you should not give any details that belong in the body of the essay.

The **thesis statement** introduces the main idea of the essay.

- It states the specific topic of the essay.
- It may list the subtopics of the main topic.
- It may also mention the method of organization.
- It is the last sentence of the introduction.

Reread the introductory paragraph of the model essay "The Computer Revolution." Notice how the sentences gradually move from the general topic of technology to the specific topic of two areas that have been changed by personal computers. This introductory paragraph resembles a funnel, wide at the top (beginning) and narrow at the bottom (end).

> We live in the age of technology. Every day, new technology appears, ranging from mini-CDs that contain entire encyclopedias of information to giant space telescopes that can send photographs of distant stars back to Earth. Of all the new technological wonders, personal computers have probably had the greatest influence on the daily lives of average people. Through computers, we can now talk to people in any country, research any topic, work, shop, bank, and entertain ourselves. Personal computers have especially revolutionized communication and business practices in the past twenty years.

- The first two sentences introduce the general topic of technology. The mini-CDs and giant telescopes are mentioned to attract the reader's interest.
- The next two sentences narrow the general topic of technology to the specific topic of personal computers. The details keep the reader interested without revealing the essay contents.
- The final sentence is the thesis statement. It names the two subtopics or specific areas changed by personal computers: communication and business.

Practice The Introductory Paragraph

In the following introductory paragraphs, the sentences are in incorrect order. Rewrite each paragraph on a separate sheet of paper, beginning with the most general statement first. Then add each sentence in correct order, from the next most general to the least general. Finally, write the thesis statement last.

1. (1) therefore, workaholics' lifestyles can affect their families, social lives, and health. (2) Because they work so many hours, workaholics may not spend enough time in leisure activities. (3) Nowadays, many men and women work in law, accounting, real estate, and business. (4) These people are serious about becoming successful; they work long hours during the week and even on weekends, so they are called "workaholics."
2. (1) Therefore, anyone who wants to drive must carry a driver's license. (2) It is divided into four steps: studying the traffic laws, taking the written test, learning to drive, and taking the driving test. (3) Getting a driver's license is a complicated process. (4) Driving a car is a necessity in today's busy society, and it is also a special privilege.
3. (1) During this period, children separate themselves from their parents and become independent. (2) Teenagers express their separateness most vividly in their choice of clothes, hairstyles, music, and vocabulary. (3) The teenage years between childhood and adulthood are a period of growth and separation.

Body Paragraphs

The body of the essay is made up of one or more paragraphs. Each of these paragraphs has a topic sentence, supporting sentences, and sometimes a concluding sentence. Each of the **body paragraphs** supports the thesis statement.

Read the two body paragraphs of the model essay on pages 87–88. The topic sentence of each paragraph introduces an area that has been changed by personal computers. Then each topic sentence is followed by several sentences that give specific examples of the changes.

THESIS STATEMENT

Personal computers have especially revolutionized communication and business practices in the past twenty years.

TOPIC SENTENCES

- Perhaps the most important effect of personal computers has been to expand our ability to communicate with the outside world.
- Besides improving communication, personal computers have made it possible to do business from home.

Practice Topic Sentence for Body Paragraphs

For the thesis statements below, write topic sentences for supporting body paragraphs. Follow the preceding example. Begin each topic sentence with an order-of-importance or additional idea transition signal (first, in addition, *etc.*).

1. Young people who live at home have several advantages.

   a. ______________________________

   b. ______________________________

   c. ______________________________

2. Owning a car is a necessity for several reasons.

   a. ______________________________

   b. ______________________________

   c. ______________________________

3. Women are superior to men in two ways.

   a. ______________________________

   b. ______________________________

The Concluding Paragraph

The conclusion is the last paragraph of the essay. It does three things:

- It signals the end of the essay.
- It summarizes the main points.
- It leaves the reader with the writer's final thoughts on the subject.

Just as the introductory paragraph has two parts, the general statements and the thesis statement, the concluding paragraph has two parts, the concluding sentences and the final thoughts.

Concluding Sentence(s)

The first part of the concluding paragraph summarizes the main points or repeats the thesis statement in different words. This may require one or more than one sentence. The first sentence of a concluding paragraph sometimes, but not always, begins with a conclusion transition signal such as *In brief* or *In short*. It is not always necessary to use a conclusion signal, and you should avoid the overused phrases *In conclusion* and *In summary*.

THESIS STATEMENT

Personal computers have especially revolutionized communication and business practices in the past twenty years.

CONCLUDING SENTENCES

In brief, the computer age has arrived, and it is changing our lives. Computers have made communicating and doing business faster and more convenient, and they have greatly increased our access to information.

Final Thoughts

In the second part of the concluding paragraph, you may write your final comments on the subject of your essay. This is the place to express your opinion, make a judgment, or give a recommendation. However, do not add any new ideas in the conclusion because it is the end of your essay. Just comment on what you have already discussed.

MODEL ESSAY: ESSAY ORGANIZATION

Read the model essay and answer the questions that follow it.

The Computer Revolution

We live in the age of technology. Every day, new technology appears, ranging from mini-CDs[1] that contain entire encyclopedias to giant space telescopes that can send photographs of distant stars back to Earth. Of all the new technological wonders, personal computers have probably had the greatest influence on the daily lives of average people. Through computers, we can now talk to people in any country, research any topic, work, shop, bank, and entertain ourselves. Personal computers have especially revolutionized communication and business practices in the past twenty years.

Perhaps the most important effect of personal computers has been to expand our ability to communicate with the outside world. A lonely invalid[2] in Minnesota can talk with a similarly house-bound[3] person in Mississippi. Schoolchildren in Manhattan can talk via computer to schoolchildren in Moscow. A high school student can obtain statistics for a history paper from a library in London. A single computer user can send an e-mail[4] message to millions of people all over the world with one keystroke.[5] Computer users can get together in an on-line[6] "chat room"[7] to discuss their interests and problems with others who have similar interests and problems. For example, a person whose hobby is collecting antique guns can share information with other gun collectors via computer. A person who is

[1]**mini-CD:** small compact disk; [2]**invalid:** sick person; [3]**house-bound:** having to stay inside the house; [4]**e-mail:** electronic mail; [5]**keystroke:** pressing of a key, or button, on a computer keyboard; [6]**on-line:** by modem (a piece of equipment that connects computers by means of telephone lines); [7]**chat room:** on-line place where computer users "talk" to many people at the same time

planning a vacation and wants to know the names of the best beaches in Hawaii can ask others who have already been there for suggestions. People even start on-line romances in chat rooms! The possibilities of computerized communication are indeed unlimited.

Besides improving communication, personal computers have made it possible to do business from home. You can take care of personal business. For example, you can buy airline tickets, send flowers to a friend, pay your bills, buy and sell stocks, and even pay your taxes from your home computer at any time of the day or night. This is a great convenience for people who are busy during the day and for physically disabled people who find it hard to leave their homes. Moreover, telecommuting–working at home instead of going to the office–has become a choice for thousands of business people. Suzanne Carreiro, a financial manager for a large company in downtown Manhattan, has telecommuted from her home in New Jersey for the past two years. She goes to her office only once a week. Four days a week, she works at home and communicates with her staff by computer. She says, "I am much more productive when I work at home because there are no interruptions. I also don't have to spend three hours traveling to and from the office every day. I save myself time, and I save my company money by telecommuting."

In brief, the computer age has arrived, and it is changing our lives. Computers have made communicating and doing business faster and more convenient, and they have greatly increased our access to information. Just as the invention of automobiles had an unplanned consequence–the growth of suburbs–so will the invention of personal computers. We will have to wait and see what these unintentional[8] consequences will be.

Questions on the Model

1. According to this essay, what two areas have computers changed?
2. Find two sentences, one in the first paragraph and one in the last paragraph, that name both of these areas. Double underline them.
3. Underline the topic sentences of the two middle paragraphs.

---

[8]**unintentional:** unplanned

Appendix C

Punctuation

Reviewing the Rules

Academic writing follows certain generally accepted rules of punctuating with periods, commas, and semicolons. Below is a list of abbreviations that will be used to discuss the rules of punctuation.

ic = independent clause, or sentence (a group of words that contains a subject and a verb and that can stand alone)
cc = coordinating conjunction *(for, and, nor, but, or, yet, so)*
t = transition (e.g., *however, moreover, therefore*)
ac = adverbial clause (begins with a subordinating conjunction)
z = anything which is the same grammatical structure

Using Commas

- With Coordinating Conjunctions

When a coordinating conjunction connects two independent clauses, use a comma before the conjunction.

Ic, cc ic.

Example Jonas is very shy, so he never goes to parties.

- With Transitions

Use a comma around a transition no matter where it appears in a sentence (at the beginning, in the middle, or at the end).

T, ic.
Ic [first part], t, ic [second part].
Ic, t.

Examples Jonas is very shy. <u>However,</u> his brother is an extrovert.
Jonas is very shy. His brother, <u>however,</u> is an extrovert.
Jonas is very shy. His brother is an extrovert, <u>however</u>.

- With Adverbial Clauses

  Use a comma after an adverbial clause preceding the subject of an independent clause. However, if the adverbial clause comes after the independent clause, don't use a comma.

  Ac, ic.
  Ic ac.

Examples Because Jonas is very shy, he never goes to parties.
Jonas never goes to parties because he is very shy.

There is an exception to this rule. When an adverbial clause beginning with the subordinators *whereas* or *while* comes after an independent clause, use a comma.

Examples Whereas Jonas is very shy, his brother is an extrovert.
Jonas' brother is an extrovert, whereas Jonas is very shy.

- In Lists

  Use commas to separate three or more items in a list. Note that the comma before the word *and* is optional.

  z, z, and z
  OR
  z, z and z

Examples We had meat, potatoes, and corn for dinner.
Tom went to the University of Illinois because he liked the climate, admired its professors, and thought highly of its medical school.
My favorite classes are English, history and biology.

Using Semicolons

Two independent clauses which are closely connected in meaning may be connected with a semicolon. In addition, transitions joining two independent clauses may be preceded by a semicolon and followed by a comma.

Ic; ic.
Ic; t, ic.

Examples Jonas is very shy; he never goes to parties.
Jonas is very shy; therefore, he never goes to parties.

Punctuation Problems

Both native and non-native speakers of English make three common errors in punctuating sentences: fragments, comma splices, and run-on sentences.

Fragments

A **fragment** is a phrase or a part of a sentence that is incomplete. The minimum sentence in English must contain a subject and a verb with a tense. (Imperatives are special cases.) Four common fragment problems are:

1. a dependent clause
   Example Because it was hot outside.

2. a phrase without a verb with a tense

   Example John going to the store.

3. a phrase without a subject

   Example Went to the store yesterday.

4. a noun phrase without a verb

   Example An air-conditioned car.

   These fragment problems can be solved in the following ways:

1. attach the dependent clause to an independent clause

   Correction: John drove to the store because it was hot outside.

   OR

   Because it was hot outside, John drove to the store.

2. change the verb form to include a tense

   Correction: John was going to the store.

3. add a subject

   Correction: John went to the store yesterday.

4. add a verb and decide if the noun phrase is the subject or object

   Correction: John has an air-conditioned car.

Comma Splices

A **comma splice** occurs when a comma is used by itself between two independent clauses.

Example I went to my friend's house, he wasn't home.

There are four common ways to correct comma splices:

1. substitute a period for the comma

   Correction: I went to my friend's house. He wasn't home.

2. substitute a semicolon for the comma

   Correction: I went to my friend's house; he wasn't home.

3. add a coordinating conjunction

   Correction: I went to my friend's house, but he wasn't home.

4. change one of the clauses to a dependent clause by starting it with a subordinating conjunction

   Correction: Even though I went to my friend's house, he wasn't home.

Run-on Sentences

A **run-on sentence** occurs when two or more independent clauses (plus possible dependent clauses) follow each other without punctuation. Run-ons must be separated into independent and dependent clauses and punctuated properly.

Example I didn't have enough milk in the house yesterday so I went to the store to buy some the store was closed so I drove to my friend's house but he wasn't at home I decided not to eat breakfast.

To correct a run-on sentence, add commas and periods.

Correction: I didn't have enough milk in the house yesterday, so I went to the store to buy some. The store was closed, so I drove to my friend's house, but he wasn't at home. I decided not to eat breakfast.

Punctuation Exercise 1

Complete the punctuation of this letter containing adjective phrases and clauses.

September 30
Dear Mom and Dad,

Thanks again for bringing me down here to the university last weekend. Classes didn't start until Wednesday so I had a few days to get adjusted. I'm signed up for five classes: zoology calculus English and two history sections. It's a heavy load but they're all courses that will count for my degree. The zoology class which meets at 8:00 every morning is going to be my hardest subject. The history class that I have in the morning is on Western civilization the one that I have in the afternoon is on early U.S. history. Calculus which I have at noon every day looks like it's going to be relatively easy. Besides zoology the other class that's going to be hard is English which we have to write a composition a week for.

I like all of my roommates but one. There are four of us in our suite including two girls from Texas and a girl from Manitoba. Sally who is from San Antonio is great I feel like I've known her all my life. I also really like Anne the girl from Manitoba. But Heather the other girl rom Texas is kind of a pain. She's one of those types of people who never tell you what's bothering them and then get hostile. All in all though it looks like it's going to be a great year. I'll write again in a week or so.

Love,
Vicky

Punctuation Exercise 2

Read the following paragraph. Correct the eight fragments by joining them to the independent clauses to which they are logically connected. Where necessary, add commas and change capitalization, but do not add words.

The life of Stella and Hank Wong has improved immeasurably. Since they both got new jobs. Stella got a position as a proofreader and editor at a publishing company. That is pioneering new workplace methods. Hank was hired as a full-time consultant for an engineering firm. The difference between their new jobs and their old ones can be summed up in one word: flextime. Until they secured these new positions. Stella and Hank had a very difficult time raising their two small children. Their life was extremely stressful. Because they were at the mercy of a nine-to-five schedule and had to pay a lot for day care. In order to get to work on time. They had to have the children at the day care center by 7:30 every morning. Each of their new companies, however, offers a flextime schedule. As long as Stella and Hank put in their 40 hours a week. They are free to work. When it is convenient for them. Now they can take turns staying home with the children, and day care is just a memory. Best of all, the children are much happier. Because they are getting the attention they need.

Appendix D

Common Linking Words

	Transitions	Conjunctions		Prepositions
		Subordinators	Coordinators	
Chronology	first, second, etc. first of all at first next after that later on at last finally then eventually	after before while when since	and or	after before since prior to
Description	nearby			on top of under to the left to the right in front of behind above next to
Example	for example for instance			such as
Causation		because since as	for	because of due to

	Transitions	Conjunctions		Prepositions
		Subordinators	Coordinators	
Result	therefore for this reason as a result/ consequence consequently hence			
Unexpected Result	however nevertheless nonetheless	even though although	but yet	in spite of despite
Contrast	however in contrast		but yet	in contrast to instead of different from
Direct Contrast	on the other hand however	whereas while	but yet	unlike
Similarity	likewise similarly in the same way		both . . . and neither . . . nor not only . . . but also	like similar to
Explanation Emphasis	in other words that is indeed in fact			
Addition	in addition furthermore moreover			in addition to
Condition	otherwise in this case	if		
Conclusion	in conclusion to sum up in short all in all